Raising a Reader

Simple and Fun Activities for Parents to Foster Reading Success

Bonnie D. Schwartz

ScarecrowEducation
Lanham, Maryland • Toronto • Oxford
2003

Published in the United States of America
by ScarecrowEducation
An imprint of The Rowman & Littlefield Publishing Group, Inc.
4501 Forbes Boulevard, Suite 200, Lanham, Maryland 20706
www.scarecroweducation.com

PO Box 317
Oxford
OX2 9RU, UK

British Library Cataloguing in Publication Information Available

Library of Congress Cataloging-in-Publication Data

Schwartz, Bonnie D.
  Raising a reader : simple and fun activities for parents to foster reading
success / Bonnie D. Schwartz.
      p. cm.
  Includes bibliographical references.
  ISBN 1-57886-051-2 (pbk. : alk. paper)
  1. Reading (Early childhood) 2. Reading—Parent participation. I. Title.
LB1139.5.R43 S37 2003
372.4—dc21

                                                        2003008376

⊗™ The paper used in this publication meets the minimum requirements of
American National Standard for Information Sciences—Permanence of
Paper for Printed Library Materials, ANSI/NISO Z39.48-1992.
Manufactured in the United States of America.

Contents

Acknowledgments

This book is a culmination of many years as a teacher and learner. I am grateful to my mother, Dorothy Ann Schwartz, who was such an excellent and patient mother and teacher. Many of the ideas for songs and activities in this book were inspired by memories of my early years with my mother. Her oral stories, fairy tales, songs, and poems encouraged me to be a reader. Parents who share the love of music and reading are wonderful gifts to their children.

I am also grateful to my daughter, Jessica Lynn Mikes, who has been a willing guinea pig her entire life. Every idea or strategy I was exposed to was practiced on her. We waded through piles of books, sang a few million songs, played the games presented in this book (and more), and made a lot of road trips! I am proud to say that she has become a wonderful lifelong reader and learner, and I am delighted that she is studying to be an English teacher.

To every student I have ever had the pleasure of teaching, from preschool to high school, thank you for teaching me. To every teacher I have had the privilege of working with and learning from—from kindergarten teachers to current professors—I am eternally indebted. I am amazed at the vast knowledge that we can find in these dedicated professionals. There is no greater occupation. Where else can you read, play, sing, hang out with kids, and learn—and get paid?

This book would never have been finished without the help of my great friend and proofreader, Mike Houck. Thank you for asking me if I worked on the book almost every day during the last month of writing. The constant encouragement was ego-boosting. I especially appreciate the painstaking efforts to read every word for content, agreement, and punctuation. No one could be a better friend and supporter. Mike also introduced me to his sister-in-law, Mari Houck, who did some of the proofing. It was the most comprehensive, detail-oriented proofreading I have ever experienced. Mari is talented! Thank you.

I would also like to thank Dr. Robert Brown, one of the outstanding professors at the University of St. Thomas. Dr. Brown introduced me to the editorial staff at ScarecrowEducation. That introduction was the beginning of my journey into the world of writing.

Finally, I would like to express my gratitude to all teachers devoted to the teaching of reading who have taken their time to share their research and best practices with the rest of the world. Their work has been an inspiration to me, as well as a resource for inspiring ideas.

Introduction

Children who are read to from an early age are more successful at learning to read.

— W. Teale

Recent research into human brain development is proving that parents truly are their children's first teachers. What parents do, or don't do, has a lasting impact on their child's reading skill and literacy. For example, there is considerable evidence of a relationship between reading regularly to a child and that child's later reading achievement.

— National Research Council

There have been so many discussions and theories about reading and how children learn to read that it all can be very confusing. There are some simple research- and practice-proven approaches that a parent can do to promote literacy in the home and encourage children to explore the great adventures to be found in books. The first step in fostering literacy and good reading strategies in the home is to learn a little bit about how language is acquired and how this affects the development of reading. The first two chapters of this book focus on building some backround knowledge and savvy vocabulary so parents can successfully fulfill their role as their child's first and most critical reading teacher.

After building a knowledge base, it is important to become equipped with some tools and strategies. Chapters 3–6 expose you to games, activities, materials, and resources to share with your child and guide him or her along the path of learning. It is important to share experiences and cultivate enthusiasm about all the components that join together to create the world of a reader. You are the mentor who will lead your new reader to a whole new world of sounds, rhythms, and words. As your child develops and grows as a reader, you can use the included comprehension techniques and strategies to help him or her achieve maximum understanding of the story and its meaning.

An important part of learning is assessment. How do I know if what I am doing is working effectively? Chapters 7 and 8 expose you to user-friendly tools and checklists to monitor your child's progress. These tools can help identify areas of strength and also highlight areas to focus on to insure continued growth.

You have made an important and life-changing decision for your child. Your effort and enthusiasm in raising your reader will have unlimited benefits as your child grows and learns. Recognizing the important role reading plays in our lives and in the whole world is the first step. Your commitment will provide the best possible example for your child.

CHAPTER 1

The Basics

You are about to embark on a magical journey that will take you places you have never dreamed that you would or could ever go. You are a parent. You have decided to become the mentor, teacher, advisor, protector, and for at least the first few years, the center of your child's world. A major part of this journey will be guiding your child along the path to lifelong reading. Empowering your child with this precious gift will provide him or her with the key to unlocking adventures, mysteries, and a myriad of knowledge in the real world and within his or her imagination. With such a task at hand, how do you begin?

The first step is understanding what reading is and how reading is learned. Any dictionary will tell you that reading is the ability to examine and grasp the meaning of written or printed characters, words, or sentences. It seems pretty simple, doesn't it? The extremely complex process of developing into a reader is often taken for granted.

Reading is a meaning-making process. While your eyes scan the page, your brain is making lots of connections. Your optic nerve is sending visual messages to your brain. Your brain is decoding the letter symbols that make up the words by accessing the phonemic knowledge you have stored. It blends the letters into words and creates sentences. Meanwhile, your long- and short-term memory activates, seeking to make connections between the information on the page and what you have learned in your life. Simultaneously, your brain is asking questions about what you are reading and making predictions about what may happen next.

Basically, learning to read is the culmination of an intricate process of language acquisition (learning to speak and understand language), phonemic awareness (hearing and recognizing that individual sounds are used to create words), and life experiences.

Well, what exactly is language acquisition? Over the years research has shown us that reading is much more than just examining and grasping meaning. Reading is the ability to decode and understand the complex system of our written language. It requires a solid understanding of the semantics (the meaning) and syntax (the rules) of our language. Researchers have discovered that children recognize and understand between 10,000 and 16,000 words by the time they begin formal reading instruction. This breaks down to two to four new words for every day of a child's life!

How does language acquisition translate into reading? Over the past twenty years, there has been a lot of research dedicated to understanding the process of how people learn to read. There has been controversy about whether children learn to read naturally or need a systematic regime of phonics and progressive skills. Even the government jumped on the bandwagon. On January 8, 2002, President Bush signed the "No Child Left Behind Act," which states that all children should be reading at grade level by the end of third grade.

There have been evolutions and even a few revolutions, but I will spare you the specifics. The bottom line is that through this process, we have uncovered some clear and fundamental truths about reading and how children learn to read. These can be translated into some pretty basic and sound principles that parents can easily use and adapt for their homes.

Begin at the beginning. The first thing to realize is that language has oral, written, and physical components that work together. While children are forming in the womb, they experience the rhythms and patterns of spoken language in a very physical way. At birth, the world of sound opens a new dimension of our language. They begin to recognize the voices of parents and loved ones. Certain sounds, words, and even music become familiar and connect to specific meanings. As they begin to speak, they realize that certain sounds linked together can result in desired responses. A short cry can result in being fed. A wail can alert mom or dad that a diaper needs changing. These noises evolve into words, and the development of language is on its way.

Learning to read is built upon the foundation of language acquisition. Researchers have assigned names for the different components of reading development. Phonemic awareness is recognizing and using individual sounds to create words. It is also understanding that words are made up of different sounds put together to create meaning. Phonemic awareness is the component of reading that becomes the foundation for building good readers. The goal of this book is to share ideas about how a child can build this foundation and to inspire parents to create an environment for their children to grow to be the best possible readers they can be.

The meaning of text does not lie in the words on the page. Readers create meaning as they decode the words and messages of the text by making connections to their own lives and experiences. Researchers have discovered that information and learning are stored in the long-term memory. As memory or "prior knowledge" is activated and linked with the text, meaning is constructed and new learning occurs. The effectiveness of this ability to assimilate past learning with new experiences depends on "metacognitive" skills. *Metacognition* is a scientific word that basically means the ability to think about, monitor, and control learning by adapting and revising strategies to get the most meaning possible out of everything that is read.

Reading, language, and writing development are all interrelated (see figure 1.1). In order to become strong readers, it is important to develop in these four areas: reading, writing, listening, and speaking. In most

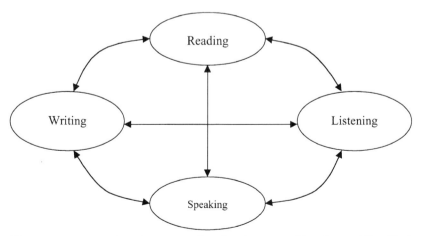

Figure 1.1.   *Interrelationship between Reading, Language (Listening and Speaking), and Writing.*

cases, we learn to listen first. Through hearing the sounds and words of others, we begin to speak. As we develop language, listening, and oral communication skills, we build a strong foundation for reading development. As we become stronger readers, language and writing abilities strengthen. Readers can also increase their comprehension strategies through writing. Writing helps to increase the understanding of how language is constructed and how text can flow.

It pays to start early. Research shows that children who are ready to read when they start school and read well in the early grades are far more successful in later years. As obvious as that sounds, we often take the importance of reading in our everyday lives for granted. Take an hour of your day and count the number of minutes you spend reading. Whether you are driving down the highway and reading billboards and road signs or looking up a phone number in the telephone directory, you are reading. Reading is arguably one of the most important things you will ever learn in life. So, if the research shows that learning early has advantages, it makes sense to start out early.

Reading is not a simple process. The day you decide to become a parent is the first moment to think about your child as a reader. This may seem a bit premature, but reading is an essential part of having a happy, comfortable, and productive life. It makes sense to make reading a part of your entire parenting plan. When you decide to be a parent, you are making a commitment to create, nurture, and raise a productive member of society and the world. That's huge!

For the first phase of your child's life, you are it. A parent is a child's first teacher. Parents introduce their children to spoken language. In the same manner, parents can help lay a solid foundation for children as they learn how to read written language. Parents can understand the basics of learning to read and can use ordinary, day-to-day opportunities as lessons in reading. You are the life-giver, teacher, comforter, protector, nurturer—you're it! If you feel a little bit nervous, that's a good thing. While having children is one of the most natural parts of human existence, it is also one of the most challenging. So now, you have made that choice, and time is of the essence. The purpose of this book is not to tell you how to be the best parent you can be. The goal of this book is to provide you with some insights into being the best possible nurturer of a future reader. The rest of the parental job is up to you.

After exploring the process of reading acquisition during the first six years of development, I want to briefly touch upon the next six years of your child's life and development. This information will guide you in selecting techniques, books, and resources to create the best possible environment for raising a lifelong reader. Understanding the basic language and the process of reading development will help you to understand your child's needs as a learner. These are generalities. You may find that your child is moving along at a different pace than is outlined here. That's fine. This is just a guide, not the rule.

The first phase: prebirth. The first chapter of a reader's life actually happens in the womb. A fetus lives in a warm, protected world, suspended in amniotic fluid, which moves with the rhythm and pace of the mother. I suggest that prebirth is the perfect time to establish a good family reading habit. Choose a thirty-minute block of time that you can consistently commit to each day. Find a comfortable place—the living room couch or your bedroom—where you, your partner, and other family members can sit together and share time with your baby. Remove potential distractions. Turn off cell phones, radios, and televisions. Focus on devoting those thirty minutes to your baby. Reading, singing, speaking, and listening to music are great activities. The purpose of this family time has three main purposes:

1. *Routine*. Setting aside a specific span of time each day requires a commitment but may also develop into a habit. This habit can carry on after the birth and develop into a family tradition. Research shows that children who are read to thirty minutes each day become more successful readers.

2. *Recognition*. Research indicates that babies can recognize the sound of their parents' voices. Infants respond positively to recorded sounds of their parents. Planning daily time with your baby will promote this bond. In addition, the changes in volume, rhythm, and cadence as you speak, read, sing, and communicate with your child can expose your baby to the natural patterns of our language.

3. *Relationships*. Communicating directly with your baby may help you make a stronger emotional connection before he or she makes the birth appearance. Perhaps more importantly, it creates

a daily opportunity for you and your spouse to bond together as parents and become prepared for the next twenty years of your lives.

(Special Note: Before the big event, there is someone you need to get to know: your local children's librarian. This invaluable expert can save you time and energy in seeking out great children's literature and resources. For the next six years, this person may become one of your best friends. Take the time to introduce yourself and share your goal of raising a reader. If you do not make a special connection, try another nearby library or bookstore. Having a friend who knows about children's books is a vital parental tool!)

The second phase: infancy. Your baby has arrived! As prepared as you may have felt *before* the blessed event, reality sets in. Babies are basically helpless little sponges for love and attention. At this point you will laugh at my proposal to schedule a time every day to read with your child since you are already at their beck and call 24/7. I understand your feelings, but do not surrender! Adapt this time to one of your baby's feedings. You will have a captive audience.

During the first month of development, babies can make basic distinctions in sight, sound, smell, taste, and touch (especially temperature and pain). Be sure that when you begin the reading time, you have a freshly changed, warm baby and a nice juicy bottle. Make sure you and your spouse are dressed comfortably, have removed possible distractions, and are relaxed and ready to enjoy your baby time! If you had a particularly stressful day, it is fine to take the day off. It is important to keep this a happy and comfortable part of your baby's day.

The third phase: birth to six months. During the first month or two, what you read is less important than *how* you read. A positive attitude and warm, soothing tones will make this a comforting experience for your baby. As you enter the first three or four months, color perception and visual and oral exploration will begin. Small victories, such as finally getting that big toe into the mouth, will result in elated cries, coos, and grunts of pleasure. Baby will begin to respond to hearing his or her name. This is a great time to introduce some interactive finger plays and songs. "Peek-a-boo" and "Pat-a-cake" are great icebreakers. You can add to your finger play repertoire by checking out some books at the local library. Remember, the librarian over there is your buddy now.

The fourth phase: six months to one year. Now things are starting to roll. Your baby is developing his or her own personality. Little eyes will follow your every move. Muscles will strain as tiny arms build enough strength to push a determined body up and even over. You will be delighted by smiles and gurgles and interesting grunts that you become certain are specific words with multiple meanings. The best part is the snuggly responses to your rocking and hugs of affection. Interaction with your baby is at an all-time high. This connection will only heighten as you share more and more literacy experiences together. As this time span progresses, baby will begin to manipulate books independently. This is a great time to invest in plastic, cloth, and board books.

The fifth phase: age one to two. This is the year of communication. During this phase, the constant echo of every word you utter, as your child repeats the last word of your every phrase, may unnerve you. Remember, this is a *good* thing! As speech develops, babies will begin to use one or more words to make meaning. A firm "ba" means, "Mom, I want my bottle, *now!*" You can now give simple instructions that will be understood. This is the time when the social value of speech is discovered. By the end of this year, your baby will have a vocabulary of five to twenty words. These will be mostly nouns and often identifiable only by you. Baby will enlist you in frantically energized conversations of jargon-babble, for which you will smile and nod and pretend complete understanding!

The sixth phase: the terrific twos (both *terrific* and *terrible* come from the same French word, *terrere*, "to frighten"). Parents often find this age challenging because children begin to develop a strong sense of self and identity. Communication has developed into short, mainly noun-verb sentences, which are often hard to decipher. The rhythm, fluency, pitch, and volume of language are developing consistency and control. The number one word fluctuates between *mine* and *no*. However, all these developmental processes can be guided to positive results. Your two-year-old can use his or her powers for *good!*

The seventh phase: the transformational threes. This is a very busy year. At this time of life, your child is experiencing the zenith of early development in four major areas: physical, emotional, social, and intellectual.

Baby is not really a baby anymore. Having mastered the ability to toddle, three-year-olds not only walk easily; they run, march, and even stand on one foot! At this age, children often begin to ride tricycles, feed themselves, dress themselves (although in strange and bizarre ensembles), and do many other tasks with dexterity.

At this time, children can comfortably handle books and begin to write. Pencils, pens, crayons, markers—it doesn't matter which tool they use. Encourage writing at every opportunity. Be careful to provide a lot of paper for your artist and watch diligently. Many walls bear the reminiscent scrawls of early writers. Scribbles and scratches take on meaning as children begin to make lists, write stories, and even create books of their own.

Children at this age generally exhibit an easygoing attitude with a strong sense of self and a tremendous quest for adventure. Three-year-olds are very social, enjoy brief activities with other children, take turns, and love to "help." Speaking in short sentences, a three-year-old has a vocabulary of about nine hundred words. They can tell simple stories, sing songs, and recite nursery rhymes.

The eighth phase: fantastic fours. Motor development is underway, and four-year-olds can hop and jump, cut with scissors (well, sort of), run quickly and with purpose, and throw a ball with relative accuracy. Children at this age enjoy writing their names frontward and backward! Although four-year-olds feel self-confident, they often test the boundaries. This is a highly social age when children love to play games of tag and "duck-duck-goose." By now, they have mastered from fifteen hundred to sixteen hundred words. They can ask seemingly endless questions about simple things as well as things you have absolutely no answer for!

The ninth phase: fabulous fives. The day your child turns five, you have been a parent for five years—more than 260 weeks, more than 1,820 days, and more than 40,000 hours! Your child knows over two thousand words well, can tell a story that lasts for (what seems like) hours, can read and write his or her name, count, and identify the basic colors, and most, if not all, of the letters of the alphabet. You have a miniature genius!

Five-year-olds tend to be home-centered: they like to associate with their parents; they enjoy responsibility and following the rules. Many have a deep concern for rules and not only follow them, but insist that others do the same. They know the difference between truth and fiction and are very interested in their environment.

Good health at all stages of growth is essential. All of these stages of early childhood are exciting and wonderful. Keep your child safely along his or her path of development by keeping regular dates with the pediatrician. It is important to know about any potential cognitive or language delays so that you can take them into consideration as your child grows. Some delays are very small, but being aware of them early on can make a tremendous difference. Regular visits to the doctor are helpful in monitoring growth and development. If you address developmental delays proactively, they may not adversely affect your child's learning. The longer you wait, the greater the gap grows. It is also important to realize that in some cases a child may need extra time and attention to learn and develop.

Early visits to the doctor can also help to identify vision and hearing problems. It is hard to tell if a child under the age of three needs glasses. Hearing and vision tests are a routine part of all checkups. In addition to possible vision and hearing problems, there are also many minor illnesses that can contribute to potential reading difficulties.

Most children will have at least one ear infection during their preschool years. Over one-fourth of children will have repeated ear infections. Ear infections are notorious for interrupting the hearing and listening development of young children. Ear infections and middle-ear fluid can affect a child's language development. Children are most likely to have ear infections between the ages of six months and two years, but ear infections continue to be a common childhood illness until the age of eight years.

Otitis media is an inflammation of the middle ear. This area behind the eardrum can swell or fill with fluid. It is one of the most common illnesses of childhood. When a child has fluid in the middle ear, the fluid reduces sound traveling through the middle ear. Sound may be muffled or not heard. Children with middle-ear fluid will generally have a mild or moderate temporary hearing loss. The sound is muffled as if you plugged your ears with your fingers. However, some children with ear infections have no change in their hearing at all.

Watch for possible indicators of hearing loss or difficulties. There are warning signs that can alert you to a possible infection. Your child may pull at his or her ear, say it hurts, become irritable and fussy, and have trouble sleeping. You may actually see some drainage coming from the ear. Sometimes ear infections go unnoticed. If a child has only one or two unnoticed infections, it may not be a problem.

During the first three years, when children have the most problems with ear infections, they are learning to speak and understand words. Because children learn by interacting with people around them, it may be harder to hear and understand speech if sound is muffled by fluid in the middle ear. Some researchers report that frequent hearing loss in children with middle-ear fluid may lead to speech and language difficulties. Because speech and language development are closely tied to reading acquisition, it is important to be sensitive to potential ear infections. It is important to pay special attention to the language development of children who have middle-ear fluid.

Your child may have mild hearing loss if he or she has trouble hearing very soft sounds, has difficulty paying attention (tough to monitor in a toddler or preschooler), shows a delayed response or no response when spoken to, says "huh?" or "what?" often, or turns up the sound on the TV or radio. If you notice any of these signs, be sure to contact your pediatrician.

Find a pediatrician or family doctor who takes the time to answer your questions. Many people feel rushed or nervous in doctors' offices, so make a list of questions before you go in for the visit. Remember, you made an appointment and waited to see the doctor. The doctor is there to examine your child *and* answer any relevant questions about your child's health. A five-minute conversation after the exam is not too great an expectation.

If you don't feel comfortable asking questions or if you feel that you have not received enough information, ask friends and relatives about their children's doctors. Find one who is willing to take a few minutes to discuss your child's development.

CHAPTER 2

Laying the Foundation: Ten Building Blocks to a Good Reading Foundation

BUILDING BLOCK 1: EXPLORATION

Provide as many opportunities as possible for your child to see, hear, and touch storybooks. I met a wonderful reading teacher who has a unique tradition. Whenever a friend gives birth or she is invited to a baby shower, she presents the new parents with eight children's picture books. This gift is accompanied by a promise that if these books, or any eight others, are read aloud to the baby every day, their child will be ready to read by the time he or she enters school. This supports my personal theory of reading aloud to and with children from conception until they no longer want to spend thirty straight minutes with you. (I assure you this will probably not occur until junior high school, at which time you will feel relief instead of rejection!)

Another fantastic innovation for reinforcing the exploration building block is touchable books. Some outstanding examples are *Pat the Bunny* (Touch and Feel Book) by Dorothy Kunhardt, Touch and Feel Board Books by Dorling Kindersley Publishing, and *Animal Kisses* by Barney Saltzberg.

BUILDING BLOCK 2: BUILDING BACKGROUND KNOWLEDGE

Make connections between characters, places, and events in stories and events in your own family life. When you plan a family day, include a book! If you are planning a picnic, bring along *The Teddy Bears' Picnic* by Jerry Garcia, a book that can be read or sung. *Picnic at Mudsock*

Meadow by Patricia Polacco is perfect for a fall picnic at the apple or-chard or pumpkin patch. *Peek-A-Zoo* by Marie Torres Cimarusti will be a hit on your zoo trip, especially for little ones who love to play peek-a-boo. This book has oversized flaps and bright illustrations.

Put family photos of outings into a scrapbook and add your own comments and stories. For the very young, write a name or single word under each photo. This will help to build a strong sight word vocabu-lary. Children will spend hours pouring over these familiar treasures.

BUILDING BLOCK 3: VISUAL CUES

Connect known sounds and words to actual objects and pictures. Re-member when a train was a "choo-choo" or a cow was a "moo"? You can help your very young child to develop letter-sound relationship knowledge and the basis of their own vocabulary by attaching a sound with a word. Be sure to follow up with the actual name of the animal or object. Point to a cow or a picture of a cow and say, "Moo, a cow says *moo*, Can you say *moo*? Can you say *cow*? What do cows say?" Songs and rhymes make excellent visual cues.

BUILDING BLOCK 4: SOUND

Develop good listening habits. Use music, poetry, finger plays, and sto-ries to strengthen listening skills. Sound is a very important and foun-dational element essential to reading development. Experiment by read-ing and singing with your child. Read selections with variations in volume, pace, inflection, and tempo. Nursery rhymes provide a myriad of opportunities to experiment with sound. When reading a story with dialogue, be sure to speak with a different intonation for each character.

Books that use alliteration (repetition of the same first sound), like *Annie Ate Apples: A Lift-The-Flap, Pull-The-Tab, Turn-The-Wheel, Pop-Up Alphabet Book* by Lynette Ruschak or *Aster Aardvark's Al-phabet Adventures* by Steven Kellogg, are great ways to build aware-ness of phonemic sounds. Great stories with repetitive words and phrases bring familiarity to the reading experience. Children love books like *Good Night Moon* by Margaret Wise Brown and *Brown Bear, Brown Bear, What Do You See?* by Bill Martin Jr., which have patterns that repeat over and over, until the listener can chime in with the reader. The predictable text makes it easy for children to join in the reading.

BUILDING BLOCK 5: RHYTHM AND RHYME

Create opportunities to use hands, feet, instruments, and dance to experience the rhythm of music and poetry. Children love to create noise and rhythm. Leave the door to your pots and pans cupboard open and just see what happens! Rhythm instruments are a big hit and can keep even the most squirmy child focused on listening when he or she is providing the beat to a song or rhyme. Even babies like opportunities to clap. Pull out your favorite nursery rhymes and make some noise!

A "must have" item for all parents of young children is *The Real Mother Goose* illustrated by Blanche Fisher Wright. There are many other excellent Mother Goose books, but this is a basic, well-illustrated collection of the most common rhymes. *The Completed Hickory Dickory Dock* by Jim Aylesworth and *Three Little Kittens* by Paul Galdone take readers of traditional nursery rhymes on a whole new journey. The cadence of the natural rhythms elicited from nursery rhymes and the quaint, old-fashioned language create a fun experience for children and a nostalgic one for mom and dad.

Finger plays are another great source for finding great literature with rhythmic qualities. Author Joanna Cole has compiled a number of resources for famous and familiar finger plays, children's songs, and street rhymes. Some of the best are *Pat-A-Cake and Other Play Rhymes*, *The Eentsy, Weentsy Spider: Fingerplays and Action Rhymes*, and *Miss Mary Mack and Other Children's Street Rhymes* coauthored by Stephanie Calmenson.

Children love rhyming books. Go to a library or a bookstore and walk over to a bin of children's picture books. I'm willing to bet that at least half of the books you find will be rhyming books.

BUILDING BLOCK 6: LANGUAGE

Talk, sing, read, recite, and discuss words and phrases to build a rich vocabulary. Word recognition and comprehension are key components of reading. The broader a vocabulary base children possess when they enter school, the easier time they will have making connections between the words they have learned through listening and speaking and the words they see in print.

The best way to develop a strong vocabulary is to speak, listen, and read. Prior to reading acquisition, a child learns vocabulary by listening and speaking. Introduce new and interesting words to your child. Talk about how big words like "together" have little words inside of them (*to*, *get*, *her*). Make up rhyming games that change the first letter of a word to create a new meaning. *Cat* becomes *bat* and *sat* and *mat* and *vat*. Explain how some things have many names. For example, a father is also a *dad*, a *man*, a *husband*, and so on.

BUILDING BLOCK 7: ALPHABET

Speak, sing, and experience the alphabet through games, songs, and hands-on activities. Alphabet knowledge, the ability to recognize and name the letters of the alphabet, has been identified as an important reading readiness skill for decades. Early childhood educators often use alphabet recognition as a predicting assessment to determine if a child is ready to begin reading instruction. Knowing that each letter has a correlating sound or sounds indicates that a child is on the brink of actually reading.

Learning the alphabet song is a standard childhood activity, but just knowing the song doesn't guarantee understanding. Most kids think LMNOP is actually one letter! An excellent way to promote alphabet knowledge is by using alphabet books. There are hundreds of alphabet books, many by renowned illustrators.

Another way to develop alphabet knowledge is to use manipulative alphabet blocks or magnets. Manipulatives are small items that can be physically handled, like blocks or counters. You can buy these at any department store or teacher supply store. A letter a day is a fun way to build alphabet knowledge. Start with the letter *a*. Have foods that start with *a* for breakfast. Alphabet cereal, apple juice, apricot jelly, almonds can all become conversations about the letter *a* and the many sounds it can make. If you are running an errand in the car, point out the letter *a* on signs and billboards. Make up silly songs that have only words that start with *a*. Have an appetizer before lunch. Bake some *a* cookies. Whatever. Be creative. Just have an *a*-number-one day!

BUILDING BLOCK 8: WORDS

Play games to find words and create words from alphabet letters, books, household items, and things in your child's world. Researchers say that when children have a sight word vocabulary between one hundred and two hundred words, they can read most first grade materials. A sight word vocabulary is built by seeing the same words over and over. By pointing out common words in your child's world, you can create opportunities to talk about words.

Start with letters first. Ask your child to tell you the initial letter in words you see in your world. When you stop at a stop sign, ask what letters he or she sees. Then repeat the letters. Talk about the sound each letter is making and how they mix together to make a word.

BUILDING BLOCK 9: PRINT

Create connections between sounds and words. Grasping the concept that a letter has a sound and that words are created by putting sounds together is a key element in reading development. Understanding that a written letter is a symbol that represents a sound is difficult, yet most young children have a basic awareness of this concept. Anything you can do at home to build upon this concept will strengthen your child's reading foundation.

A natural way to begin is to write the names of simple household items on index cards and tape them onto the corresponding items. For example, when your child opens a door, the word *door* will be at eye level. You can point to the word and say, "door." Ask him or her what letters are in the word *door*. I recommend the special easy-to-remove poster tape sold in office supply stores to avoid permanent sticky spots.

BUILDING BLOCK 10: VALUE

Make reading a family priority. Model good literacy habits. I received a pin at a conference for reading teachers that lists the top ten things to do to help children become better readers. Each one of the ten items listed is "Read." The best way to raise a reader is to be a reader. When you cook, read the recipe aloud. When you address an envelope, speak the words as you write them. Visit the library often. Make a shopping trip to the bookstore seem like a trip to Disney World. Make reading dates with your child. Go to a local coffee shop and have some cocoa and share a story. I could make an endless list, but I think you have the idea. Read. Read. Oh, and read!

Tools and Strategies: Activities, Literature, and Music and Movement

TEN GREAT ACTIVITIES TO DEVELOP GOOD READERS

Number 1: Listening Game

Combine good listening habits with visual awareness development by connecting directions given in song with picture cards, toys, or stuffed animals. Gather some animal pictures or toys. Put the items on a table. Sit across from your child. Use the music to the familiar song, "London Bridge," to sing these directions:

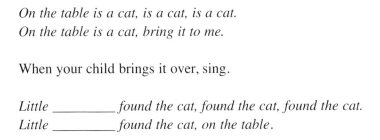

On the table is a cat, is a cat, is a cat.
On the table is a cat, bring it to me.

When your child brings it over, sing.

Little _____ found the cat, found the cat, found the cat.
Little _____ found the cat, on the table.

Number 2: Rhythm: Musical Maestro

Using rhythm sticks, play instruments, or kitchen items, beat rhythmic patterns to sentences or poems. For example, say: "I *think* that *it* is *time* for *lunch*." Use your instrument to make a beat on every other word. You can do this anytime, anywhere, with ordinary objects.

Number 3: Rhyme Day

Create a tradition and have a Rhyme Day. Turn everything into a rhyme. Whenever you speak, make sure the last word of every sentence rhymes. For example:

Good morning to you it's a beautiful day.
We're going to rhyme and play today.
Jump on up and wash your face.
Then we can have a rhyming race.

See how long you can go without missing a rhyme. Your little one will love it. Take opportunities to say Mother Goose rhymes and sing songs on this special Rhyme Day.

Number 4: Phonemic Awareness: Jumping Words

For this activity, you will need inexpensive white paper plates or pieces of construction paper. On some paper plates, write single alphabet letters. Write the endings of word family words on different plates. Word families are words that rhyme. They generally have the same ending (for example, *ab*, *ad*, *ag*, *am*, *an*, *at*, or *as*). Place the marked plates randomly on the floor. Explain the game by modeling. Select a paper plate with the letter *c* and say: "This is the letter *c*. The letter *c* makes the /c/ sound." (Start with hard /c/ as in *cat*.) Jump on the *ab* paper plate and say, "The letter *a* makes the short /a/ sound and the letter *b* makes the /b/ sound. Together they make *ab*. If I add the /c/ sound, I can make the word *cab*. Now, you try it with me!"

After your child gets the idea, let him or her jump from plate to plate, making words as a part of playing.

Number 5: Alphabet Fun

Collect items from around the house clearly beginning with letters of the alphabet that your child knows. Spread the items around the room. Be sure they are in clear view. Start with only five or six items: for example, a pillow, a blanket, a toy cat, a toy truck, and a toy snake. Use the melody from the song "The Farmer in the Dell":

I'm looking for a b
I'm looking for a b
Hi! Ho! The Derry-Oh
I'm looking for a b

You can help your child by saying if he or she is "hot" (near the object) or "cold" (farther from it).

You can also use this song in the car as you pass signs, stores, and farm animals. For example, as you pass a herd of cows, sing:

I'm looking for a c
I'm looking for a c
Hi! Ho! The Derry-Oh
I'm looking for a c

Remember to celebrate each victory!

Number 6: Eye-Hand Coordination

Have a box full of different sizes and colors of toy cars. Ask your child to sort them by color or by size. Collect lots of different items for sorting. Another great activity is stringing. String circular cereals that have open centers with yarn to make edible necklaces. Puzzles also help to develop coordination.

Number 7: Visual Discrimination: Pattern Hop

Reading requires the ability to recognize patterns, colors, shapes, and objects. Cut simple shapes from colored construction paper. Cut out two of each shape. Use masking tape to tape the shapes on the carpet or floor. Help your child copy the patterns by taping the same shapes in the same order, under or above what you created. Now, have him or her hop and say the name of each shape. Next, have him or her hop and identify the color of each shape.

Number 8: Tracking Skills

Tracking is the ability to follow a line of text across a page from left to right and from the top of the page to the bottom, and it is essential to reading. Use shape blocks, buttons, alphabet magnets, or other small manipulative objects. Put them in a specific order in a specific pattern. Have your child copy the pattern. String beads, different macaroni noodles, or cereals in special patterns. Have your child re-create the pattern, moving from left to right.

Number 9: Small Motor Development

The ability to control and coordinate the small muscles of the hand is usually connected to writing development. However, holding a book, turning pages, and feeling comfortable while reading are also important. Reading and writing are interconnected, so the following game is included as a reading activity

Everyone loves to play with chopsticks. This activity works best with children over three. Get some special children's chopsticks from your local Chinese restaurant. The children's varieties have connections at the top to make grasping easier. Pop a big bowl of popcorn or use cereal with large pieces. Have fun picking up the snacks with the chopsticks. Using hot dog tongs or tweezers to pick up objects is also great fun.

Number 10: Problem Solving, Reasoning, and Recall

Reading is making meaning from symbols. Any activity that re-creates this concept is a great reading activity. Memory games are awesome ways to foster this ability. You can make simple beginner memory games by gluing pairs of shapes or colors on 3×5 cards. Make two squares, two triangles, two rectangles, and two pentagons from construction paper or wrapping paper. Paste one shape on each card. Show them to your child. Talk about the shapes. Count the sides. Put them face down on the table. Take turns turning over two cards and trying to match them. By starting with just ten cards, you can slowly move on to more elaborate versions of the game.

TEN TYPES OF CHILDREN'S LITERATURE: THE JOY OF PICTURE BOOKS

Picture books are simple children's books that are accompanied by beautiful illustrations. They combine narrative text and illustration to tell a story. Some picture books are written at an easy-to-read level. Some have very challenging text and are created for parents to read aloud to their children. Any book that has less than forty pages and a picture on at least twenty of them can be considered a picture book. Basically, a picture book provides the child with a story accompanied by a visual experience. Within the category of picture book, you can find many of the other types of literature:

Number 1: Participation Books

Participation books allow children to become actively involved with the text and pictures. There are four basic kinds of participation books:

- Flaps: for example, *Where's Spot?* by Eric Hill
- Materials for touching: for example, *Pat the Bunny* by Dorothy Kunhardt
- Holes for poking fingers through: for example, *The Very Hungry Caterpillar* by Eric Carle
- Sounds: for example, *The Very Quiet Cricket* by Eric Carle or *Moo, Baa, LA LA LA* by Sandra Boynton

Number 2: Finger Plays and Nursery Songs

Finger plays combine rhythm, rhyme, and kinesthetic movements to encourage participation. Nursery songs provide opportunities for young children to relate familiar songs to the words in the text.

Number 3: Mother Goose

Mother Goose rhymes are a very special type of children's literature. These traditional verses have become part of our nation's oral tradition.

This collection of simple poetry can greatly impact beginning readers in four key ways:

- By modeling quality patterns of language
- By stimulating language development
- By being short and easily memorized
- By encouraging active participation

Number 4: ABC Books

ABC books provide practice in identifying symbols to match letter sounds. There are four types of ABC books:

- Word–picture format
- Simple narratives
- Riddles or puzzles
- Topical themes

Number 5: Counting Books

Begin with real objects like blocks or cars to show the relationship between numbers and objects. Counting books help to make the transition from concrete to visual representations of numbers. There are three kinds of counting books:

- One-to-one correspondence
- Simple concepts
- Number stories and puzzles

Number 6: Concept Books

Describe common characteristics and relationships between objects and concepts.
Popular Topics:

- Colors
- Shapes
- Opposites

Number 7: Wordless Books

Wordless books are stories told through pictures. Children can "read" the story by explaining the pictures. Reading wordless books requires the ability to comprehend the message of the picture and the sequence.

Number 8: Predictable Books

Predictable books are stories that have repetitive words, phrases, or rhymes throughout. These books are great for young readers because they often have simple plots and interactive illustrations. Predictable books may have one or more of these components:

- Repetitive language patterns
- Easy to predict plot sequence
- Familiar sequences and hierarchies
- Familiar songs and rhymes
- Environmental print

Number 9: Cumulative Books

Like predictable books, cumulative tales use repetition of words and action to create a story. Stories like *The Gingerbread Man* and *The Little Red Hen* gather characters throughout the tale to make it fun and create some rhythm and repetition for the reader. Cumulative books may have the following components:

- Cumulative tasks
- Snowballing plot events
- Actions or events building upon one another as the story progresses
- Increasing characters throughout the story
- Repetitive language around the accumulation.

Number 10: Controlled Vocabulary

As children develop a sight vocabulary, many enjoy reading books that have been designed especially for very early readers. Controlled vocabulary books can limit the following elements:

- The number of words in the story
- The number of words on each page
- The sounds presented
- The overall length of stories

These books are sometimes written using only the sight words recognized as being the one hundred most frequently used words in the written English language.

Some controlled vocabulary books are part of a learning-to-read series that uses a phonics or sight word approach to build reader confidence. Because controlled vocabulary books are reminiscent of the old "Dick and Jane" basal readers, some critics do not consider them to be true literature. They do, however, provide another opportunity for children to develop reading skills. There are also some very good children's authors whose work can fall into this category, such as Dr. Seuss's *The Cat in the Hat* and Arnold Lobel's *Frog and Toad*. (See also appendix A, "One Hundred Fantastic Children's Literature Books by Category," and appendix B, "One Hundred Great Children's Authors.")

MUSIC AND MOVEMENT: TEN GREAT EXPERIENCES TO CONNECT SOUND, RHYTHM, AND SPEECH

As your baby grows, there are some great activities to share that will help your child make connections between sound, rhythm, speech, and movement. Music and rhythm activities can help to establish reading roots. All five senses are engaged when children participate in music, rhythm, and dance activities. The most obvious sense, auditory hearing, is stimulated through music and rhythm. The kinesthetic senses are enhanced as children perform the actions to a song or finger play. Tactile experience connects a physical action with the thought process in the brain as you sing a song and act it out. Visually, children make connections to images they see, as well as pictures they create in their minds. It is important to make physical connections between language and reading. Props such as musical instruments, feathers, scarves, and ribbons can add dimension to many rhythm and movement activities.

Number 1: Bend and Stretch

Put on some soothing, wordless music. Classical music works well. Be sure it has a slow pace. Model these exercises by doing them with your child. Start by standing and reaching for the stars. Reach with your right arm. Stretch it all the way up and hold it. Now, bend to the left. Feel the pull along the right side of your body. Following the rhythm of the music, set a pace. Experience the feel of the music.

Raise your right arm again and count to ten. Feel a stretch. Repeat with the left. Raise both arms and hold. Count to ten. Now, slowly bend to the music until your arms are hanging in front of you like a rag doll. Hang for the count of ten. Put your hands on the floor and kneel. Make a stretching movement like a cat and hold it for the count of ten. Arch your back the other way. Hold for ten.

Continue stretching different muscles along with the music. This is a wonderful way to get ready for a nap. After stretching, you can lie down with your child and share an oral story in a soft, whispering voice.

Number 2: Stop and Go, Fast and Slow

This exercise is an opportunity for children to learn that they have control over their own bodies. Select some fun children's music like *The Singable Songs Collection* by Raffi, or *Early Childhood Classics: Old Favorites with a New Twist* by Hap Palmer. Use a tambourine or sticks to tap the rhythm of the song while your child moves through a series of physical movements.

Begin by explaining that you will be playing a game called "Stop and Go, Fast and Slow." The object of the game is to listen for verbal instructions while responding to the instruction with the appropriate action. You will be giving instructions to your child to move from a moving locomotor (moving your whole body across space) activity like walking, running, jumping, hopping, leaping, and galloping, to a non-locomotor (moving your whole body in place) activity like bending, stretching, twisting, turning, and shaking while in place, to a complete freeze or holding of his or her body. Use clear, one-word instructions like "hop," "twist," "jump," and "freeze."

Number 3: High Drama

Use a finger play or nursery rhyme to create a dramatic interpretation that your child can act out. Collect different costumes from garage sales and thrift shops. Visit department stores after Halloween to get inexpensive costumes. Using these props, encourage your child to act out various nursery rhymes and become the characters. This dramatic play will give children the opportunity to express their emotions and make connections to the rhymes.

Number 4: Props

Props can be used to accentuate any story, rhyme, or song. Collect filmy, colorful scarves, like the ones grandma wore to keep her hairdo from getting messy on windy days. Long, shiny ribbon can also do the job. Glue a two-foot length of satin ribbon to a small, six-inch dowel rod. Listen to various kinds of music. Encourage your child to use the scarves or ribbons to make swirling shapes while he or she feels the music.

Another wonderful activity is to use these props to tell a story. If you collect scarves or ribbon in the colors of the rainbow, you can retell the story of Noah and the flood. *All Aboard Noah's Ark!* (A Bible Story Chunky Flap Book) by Mary Josephs and *Noah's Ark* by Lucy Cousins are both great versions. Use the blue and green scarves or ribbons to act out the water rising from the flood. Use various other colors to portray characters, animals, and events. Encourage your child to use all the colors and stretch out his or her arms and wave them around at the end to be the rainbow. It's a fabulous way to retell a familiar story, get some exercise, and have fun.

Number 5: Echoes

Practice good listening skills by playing an echo game. Begin with a short poem or nursery rhyme. Say the first line. Ask your child to repeat the line. Continue until you have said the entire poem in an echo style. Try doing different voices. For example, say it in a tiny voice, a loud voice, an old voice, a cartoon voice, a cowboy voice, and so on. Set the rhymes to familiar tunes and sing them in an echo style. Say the rhymes slowly. Say them quickly. Have fun while teaching your child to listen for sound and rhythm variations.

Number 6: Jam Session

You can purchase a variety of rhythm instruments like a tambourine, drum, triangle, sticks, and maracas in toy stores, bookstores, and even party shops. I was able to buy some wonderful sets for very little money from a local party supply store. If you are saving money, use household items like the lids from pots and pans, wooden spoons, or plastic cups. You can make shakers or maracas by putting beans or rice in a Tupperware container. Chopsticks and an old coffee can with a plastic lid make a great set of drums!

Begin by choosing a favorite song or rhyme. Sing it through together. Explain that you are playing a game called "Jam Session." It's called "Jam Session" because professional musicians hold sessions to try out new rhythm and sound ideas with one another. Begin by beating a rhythm on your instrument. Ask your child to copy the sound. As he or she echoes your sound accurately, begin to add more difficult rhythms and longer patterns. This game will help to develop a strong sound awareness and rhythmic abilities.

Number 7: End Rhymes

Find songs and finger plays that have a rhyming word at the end of each line. Say each line, leaving off the last word. Create a rhythm that encourages your child to fill in the missing word on the beat.

Example: *Humpty Dumpty sat on the _____.*
Humpty Dumpty had a great _____.
All the king's horses and all the queen's _____.
Couldn't put Humpty together _____.

Brainstorm a new verse together, choosing a pattern that your child can anticipate:

Humpty Dumpty lay on the _____. (ground)
Wondering if all his pieces were _____. (found)

A boy with some paste and a girl with some _____. (glue)
Put Humpty together. He's now good as _____. (new)

Other activities and songs like "Down by the Bay" can help to develop the ability to create end rhymes. You can find children's CDs with versions of this song, too. I especially like Raffi's version from the CD, *The Singable Songs Collection*.

Down by the bay where the watermelons grow.
Back to my home, I dare not go.
For if I do, my mother will say:
"Did you ever see a bear
Combing his hair?"
Down by the bay.

Other possible endings are: "Did you ever see a llama, wearing a pajama?" or "Did you ever see a pig, wearing a wig?" and so forth.

Number 8: Mother Goose Limbo

Add a Caribbean flair to a winter day by playing Mother Goose Limbo. Sing Mother Goose tunes or pick up a selection of Mother Goose songs from the local library or bookstore. This works best if two adults can play. (If only one adult is home, stretch a length of rope or ribbon across two chairs.) Using a broom handle, rope, or yardstick as a limbo line, show your child how to arch backward and do the limbo under the limbo line. Turn on the tunes or start to sing. Encourage your child to move to the rhythm of the music or song.

Number 9: Body Beat

Get the whole body into the rhythm. Choose a variety of songs to play on a tape or CD player. Start by singing along with some songs with a strong pulse like "The Grand Old Duke of York" or "Pop Goes the Weasel." Tap, clap, or walk the beats as you sing. Exaggerate the strong pulse in the beat. After your child listens a few times, continue the rhythmic pattern, but change from clapping to tapping. Begin by tapping his or her head, then shoulders, elbows, hips, knees, and feet, and then back up the body again.

Number 10: Memory Beat

Pick a familiar song with a consistent beat the first few times you play this game. One great rhyme to use is *Jack and Jill,* by Mother Goose. Say the rhyme together, putting exaggerated emphasis on the stressed syllables:

> *Jack and Jill went up the hill*
> *To fetch a pail of water*
> *Jack fell down and broke his crown*
> *And Jill came tumbling after.*

Take out the rhythm sticks, toy drums, or tambourine. Beat the rhythm of the rhyme using the percussion instrument. Do it a number of times. See if you can do it together, while singing the rhyme quietly in your head. See if your child can do it alone.

After you have played this game with a few different songs, try a guessing game. You beat out a rhythm and have your child identify the song. Now, have him or her try it. It may take a while for your little one to get the hang of this activity. In the meantime, he or she will enjoy your multitude of wrong guesses of his or her simple rhythms!

BOOKS TO ENHANCE SOUND, RHYTHM, AND MUSIC ACTIVITIES

Ben's Trumpet by Rachel Isadora: Ben wants to be a trumpet player, but he plays only an imaginary instrument until a musician at a neighborhood club discovers him.

Making Music: 6 Instruments You Can Create by Michael Koelsch: This book shows how to use household objects to create musical instruments.

Sound Science by Etta Kaner: Use this book to discover the nature of sound through experiments, riddles, puzzles, and games.

Ty's One-Man Band by Mildred Pitts: Andro is a remarkable musician who brings irresistible music to Ty's town with just a plate, spoon, and cup.

Zin! Zin! Zin! A Violin! by Lloyd Moss: Ten instruments take their part one by one in a musical performance.

MUSIC TO ENHANCE SOUND, RHYTHM, AND MUSIC ACTIVITIES

Child's Celebration of the World by various artists

Choo Choo Boogaloo by Buckwheat Zydeco

Corner Grocery Store & Other Songs by Raffi

Did You Feed My Cow? Fred Koch Presents the Songs of Ella Jenkins by Fred Koch

Kids in Motion by Greg & Steve

Mother Goose Rocks by various artists

One Light One Sun by Raffi

One Little Sound: Fun with Phonics and Numbers by Hap Palmer

Reading Rainbow's Greatest Hits by various artists

Sing the Alphabet by Sesame Street

Singable Songs for the Very Young: Great with a Peanut-Butter Sandwich by Raffi

Teaching Peace by Red Grammer

CHAPTER 4

The Framework: Developing Decoding

Reading, like listening, speaking, and writing, is a feature of communication. Reading and writing build on the oral language skills that children begin developing long before they enter school. Oral and written language share many common features. They have the same vocabulary, the same grammar and language rules, and similar purposes. In order to read, children need to construct meaning from the printed language. In order to write, children need to learn to use printed language to convey a message. To be able to do these important elements of our communication system, children must be able to recognize in print the language that they use orally. This ability is referred to as word identification. It is also called decoding. Our written language is a code that stands for the language that we speak. Beginning readers must become familiar with this printed code and begin to connect it with the oral language they speak. Young children can understand and enjoy a book if someone reads the text to them. To understand and enjoy the book on their own, they need to learn to recognize printed words on the page as equal to those read aloud to them. You can help them to do this by understanding the areas that need development in order to make the connection between the words we say and the words we write. Developing the tools to decode the written language include phonemic awareness, exposure to environmental print reading, sight word vocabulary, sounding out skills, deciphering strategies, and encoding or spelling awareness.

PHONEMIC AWARENESS

One of the basic components of reading is the letter-sound relationship. Most people immediately think of phonics when you mention letters and sounds, but phonics is just a part of a whole physical and mental process of reading. Phonological awareness is the oral language skill that helps children learn about how sounds connect to letters (phonics). This awareness is auditory. The ability to rhyme, break words into syllables and syllables into sounds, and blend sounds and syllables together are all critical skills for early reading and spelling development. These are the elements of phonemic awareness.

Phonological awareness is different from phonics. Phonological awareness involves the auditory and oral manipulation of sounds. It mainly involves what your child hears and how he or she identifies individual sounds within words. It does not involve printed letters.

Children develop sound awareness through natural interaction with oral language, basically by listening and talking with others. The best way to develop this ability in your child is to read and sing often. Some children have a natural gift for rhyme and rhythm. Some children need more time. Be patient and have fun.

PHONEMIC AWARENESS ACTIVITIES

Alphabet Fun

The alphabet is a very important building block for reading development. Begin to help your child to experience the alphabet early. Buy anything that comes in alphabetical shapes: magnets, sponges, bath toys, blocks, stickers, food—anything that will encourage conversation about the alphabet.

The Alphabet Song

Start with the basic song. Look into your child's eyes. Use a lot of expression. Sing using different kinds of voices; vary the volume, pitch, and speed. Use letter blocks, magnets, or flashcards and hold them up as you sing each letter. Eventually, this is something your little one can do!

Alphabet Walk

Buy a disposable camera with at least twenty-eight picture possibilities. Tell your child that you are about to capture the alphabet. Name the camera "The Alphabet Catcher." Take it along with you and start looking for examples of things in the real world that start with alphabet letters. It's easier to go in order. Find something that starts with the letter *a*. Help your child take a picture of the object. Continue until you have a picture for each letter of the alphabet. For tricky letters like *x*, make an *x* out of clay or dough and take the picture. After the pictures are developed, have fun naming the items and the corresponding letters. Put them in alphabetical order, forward and backward!

My Alphabet Book

Buy a scrapbook, glue stick, and colored pencils or markers. Be sure that the scrapbook has twenty-eight or more pages. On each page, write one letter of the alphabet. Write the upper and lower case versions of the letter. On each letter page, paste magazine pictures, photos taken with your "Alphabet Catcher," and samples of your child's practice writing of the letter, until you have a full page of examples. Now, you have an amazingly personal visual connection to each alphabet letter, and your child had a great time making it!

Sound, Clap, and Clatter

Listening to sounds in words is important and helps to develop the phonemic awareness that is vital to reading development. Knowing where sounds of words begin and end can be practiced. Start by creating a stack of word cards with two or three syllables, for example, *baby*, *apple*, and *puppy*. Explain that every time your child hears a part of the word, he or she can clap. Use your child's name as an example. For additional fun, use rhythm sticks, a tambourine, or even pan lids for extra noise.

I Hear with My Little Ear

Developing active listening habits can be beneficial for your child. Playing with sounds can be a fun way to exercise this ability. Collect different stuffed animals and other objects that make distinctive sounds and begin the game. Say, "I hear with my little ear a sound that goes . . ." And make the sound for one of the objects. Ask your child to pick up the object and repeat the sound.

Rhyme Puzzles

Using a book of nursery rhymes or children's poems, read one to your child. If you can sing it to a familiar tune, try that too. After it becomes familiar, say the rhyme, but leave off the last word. Have your child chime in with the missing word.

Example: *Mary had a little _____.*
            Its fleece was white as _____.

ENVIRONMENTAL PRINT READING

Studies have shown that children are beginning to recognize signs and logos in the environment as early as eighteen months. This recognition comes from the combination of high exposure to certain words and images that are supported by verbal reinforcement. Environmental print is defined as "print within the environment of children." This print would include logos, labels, billboards, and road signs.

Children who love to visit McDonald's will come to recognize the familiar golden arches. As they are exposed more and more, they will begin to recognize the "Mc" and may make the association. Just as they recognize that they are pulling into grandma's driveway because of the familiar house, they will recognize familiar words on signs and boxes. They will know the way their favorite cereal box looks and will learn to recognize the word on the front.

Recognizing this print in the environment is one of the first signs of emerging literacy skills in young children. Environmental print recognition plays an important role in supporting children's developing knowledge about what literacy is and what it does.

ENCOURAGING ENVIRONMENTAL PRINT READING

Road Games

Whenever you are taking a walk or drive along a familiar route, play "Road Game." Select a few things along the route that have a definite picture, symbol, or word that is always related to them. A stop sign is a great thing to use. Every time you see a stop sign, stop and point. Ask your child, "What color is that sign? It's red. That is a stop sign. It is always red with white letters on it. The letters spell out the word *stop*. *Stop* is spelled, S-T-O-P." Eventually, your child will know the colors and the spelling. Eventually, the roles will reverse, and you will be the one who is being asked. Choose four or five things along your familiar route to start. When you notice that your child is beginning to recognize them, add some more.

Memory

Take pictures of the signs and symbols from your Road Game adventure. Get double copies. Write the word in marker at the bottom of the picture. Put the pictures face down. Start with just four or five different pictures. Have your child turn them over, two at a time, and try to make pairs. Talk about the pictures as you play.

Home Signs

Use 3 × 5 index cards or photographs to make labels for things around your home. Take a picture of the stove and write *stove* on the bottom. Tape it to the stove. When you are cooking, ask your child what the card says. Spell the word together. Do this with other items in the home that are used daily.

SIGHT WORD DEVELOPMENT

The concept of sight words began in the "Look-Say" approach to reading instruction. This approach is very visual. The idea is to begin teaching children to recognize the one hundred most commonly used words in print. By exposing your child to these words over and over through reading familiar texts, playing games, and using flashcards, the words become part of the child's memory and are recognized on sight. After acquiring the first one hundred words, children can begin to read very simple books. As they become more confident readers, more words can be added.

There are many sight word lists. The two best-known lists are the Dolch List and the Fry Words. Each list takes the five hundred most commonly used words in the English language and arranges them in lists of one hundred words. Many of these words are hard to sound out and don't follow typical spelling rules. Research has found that it takes at least two hundred encounters with a word for it to become part of a child's sight word vocabulary.

You can buy books and flashcards that use these lists at most bookstores. These lists are also easy to get from many Internet sites. You can use the words to create your own flash cards and games at home. Try to expose your child to four or five words at a time. As he or she masters them, add two more and continue until a base of twenty to thirty words is mastered. Try arranging the words into sentences and phrases. Look for the words in books you read aloud. Your child will begin to feel like an experienced reader as he or she is able to read words with you.

SIGHT WORD DEVELOPMENT ACTIVITIES

Books

There are many great children's books with basic sight words accompanied by a picture. Richard Scarry is an excellent example. He has created a number of large and colorful books that you can use to engage in conversations about words.

Go FISH!

Cut fish shapes out of colored paper. Write sight words from the first one hundred sight word list by Dolch or Fry in large letters on the fish. Start with five or six familiar words that are easy to sound out, such as *in*, *at*, *up*, *bat*, or *cat*. Put a paper clip on each fish. Tie a piece of yarn or string to a dowel rod or wooden spoon. Tie a magnet to the other end of the string. Ask your child to "catch" the fish that says *cat* and spell it. See how many fish your child can catch. As he or she learns, make more fish.

SOUNDING OUT WORDS (PHONICS)

The awareness of sound, a repertoire of environmental print recognition, and a good sight vocabulary are important building blocks in learning to read. They are also great indications that your child is ready for more. Phonics is learning that there are relationships between printed letters or groups of letters and their pronunciations. It is actually decoding or interpreting a word sound by sound.

Researchers have determined that for children to become competent readers they need to learn to decode words rather than simply memorizing them. Decoding words is a much easier and more flexible strategy than memorization. Children who can decode words are able to break down new, unfamiliar words by using a variety of strategies to sound them out. By examining the letters and chunks within the words and breaking them down into understandable parts, children can make sense of them.

There are twenty-six letters in our alphabet. These letters all have sounds. Some letters make more than one sound. Sometimes, two or more letters combine to make a sound. There are more than forty phonemes, or sounds, that can be made from the twenty-six letters in our alphabet. (See "What is a Phoneme?" in chapter 8.) You can help your child begin the journey into phonics learning by teaching him or her the alphabet letters and the sounds they can make.

SOUNDING OUT GAMES

Favorite Letters

Get some manipulative ABC shapes or magnetic alphabet letters. Ask your child to pick five favorite consonant letters. Pick one vowel sound. Sit on the floor or at a table (or by the refrigerator or near a magnetic surface if you have magnetic alphabet letters) and talk about the sound each letter makes. See how many words can be made out of the five favorite consonant letters and a vowel. Write the words on a piece of paper. Continue the game, changing the vowel.

Letter of the Day

Start each day with a letter of the day. Each time your child sees the letter in a word, stop and talk about the letter, the sound, and the word it is in.

Consonant Swap!

Use a wipe-off board and write a word like *at* on the board. Using manipulative ABC shapes or magnetic alphabet letters try putting different letters at the beginning of the word to see what words your child can make. A fun twist would be to use pudding or yogurt on a clean placemat. Write the word *at* in pudding on the placemat. Make as many new words that start with another letter and end with *at* as you can. Now, eat them!

DECIPHERING

I am adding the idea of deciphering to the mix. Deciphering is actually activating strategies to use phonemic awareness, exposure to environmental print reading, sight word vocabulary, sounding out skills, and phonics knowledge your child has learned and putting them all together to read words and phrases. Deciphering is putting all this learning into action. It is the growing awareness that sounds make letters and letters make sounds. Knowledge that sounds and letters make words, words make phrases, and phrases join to make sentences and paragraphs is the basis of reading our language. It is the magical coming together of everything you have been working toward from the moment you decided to raise a reader.

ENCODING

Reading is decoding or extracting the underlying meaning from the text. Encoding is putting a message into a code or writing. Learning to encode is basically just learning to spell. It just sounds more scientific. You will appreciate the fancy term as you embark on this aspect of the literacy journey. It's a long road, but it can be very, very fun.

When children first put a pencil, crayon, or pen to paper, it seldom looks like any system of writing we can recognize. Thousands of years from now, archeologists may uncover your child's first efforts and believe it to be a complex system of communication. They will be right. Even though it may just be chicken scratches on paper, your child has a purpose in every mark. He or she knows that print carries a message.

At first, your little one will not have the small motor coordination in his or her hands to write very long or in a confined space. But, if you give your child a lot of opportunity to write, paint, draw, and color, he or she will begin to have more dexterity. Scribbles will become pictures with underlying messages. Eventually, you may begin to recognize some letters mixed in. Encourage writing by leaving notes for your child and reading them aloud. Ask your child to write notes to you and have him or her read the messages. Ask your child to write your shopping list. (Be sure you know what you need. The list may change between home and the store.)

As your child begins to hold a pencil with control, teach him or her a few letters. Eventually, your child will be able to write his or her own name. Ask your child to tell you a story. Write down the words on pieces of paper, one sentence at a time. Go back and make pictures for each page. Read and reread the "book." Eventually, your child may try to write the words. He or she will also be able to "read" the book. Copying words that you have written is a good practice at this time.

Soon, your child will write down a letter or two to represent a word and will be able to "read" it back to you. The letter *r* they wrote may represent a hundred different things. What they "read" to you may change. That is fine. Actually, it's more than fine. It is totally excellent. Your child is an emerging writer!

As your child gains confidence and experience, he or she will begin to write words the way they sound. This is the encoding process. It is hearing a sound, knowing there is a letter symbol to represent it, and assigning a letter to represent that sound. Absolutely do not worry about spelling at this time. It will come. The important thing is that the connection has been made. Your child realizes that a letter is a symbol that represents a sound. That is *huge*! The awareness of this concept tells you that your child is ready to write.

Exhibit your child's writing, praise his or her writing, and do all you can to encourage it. Make sure that any paper you leave in reach is OK to write on, because your child probably will write on anything and everything available.

PUTTING IT TOGETHER: DECODING AND ENCODING

There are some great all-around activities to promote reading development. You can search through books at the library, surf the Internet, ask friends and family, and create your own. The important thing is that you do an assortment of different reading, writing, listening, and speaking activities with your child. The suggestions below may help to stimulate your own wonderful ideas.

My Ending

Sometimes, the saddest part of a book is the end because that's it, no more! Sometimes a story's ending is a big surprise, and other times it is easy to predict. You can make this an important part of learning by teaching your child that the end is not always the end! You can play this game with a new book or an old familiar book.

- New book: Read a new story. Stop reading before the ending and ask your child to tell you the ending. Then, read the author's ending. Talk about how they are the same or different.
- Familiar book: Start with a well-told tale. You can use a book or just do an oral story. Let your child tell you the story. When the end is near, ask for a new ending.

Stories Come to Life

High drama! Find a story that has a lot of verbs or action words. Read it together with your child. Talk about how some words have actions. Read the story again, but this time ask your child to act it out. Whenever you come to a verb, say it loud and pause, giving your child a chance to act it out. Take turns doing the actions. This activity will keep active children interested.

Picture Predictions

Listening to a great story and predicting what will happen next is an important part of reading. Gather some colorful paper, pens, and markers. Read a few pages from a picture book but don't show the picture. Ask your child to draw an illustration that would go with the story. You can join in, too. When you are finished, reread the story and use your child's pictures as the illustrations. Then, compare your child's pictures to the ones in the book. Talk about how they are the same or different.

Another slant on this idea is to use a wordless picture book. Peter Spier illustrates some excellent wordless books that are great to use. Go through the pictures with your child and talk about what you see. Then, go back through the illustrations and ask your child to tell you the story. Record his or her story on tape or write it down. Replay or retell the story!

TV Time

Television and videos are a big part of the lives of most children. Why fight it! Let's use it. Before watching a show together, video-tape it. Get the biggest piece of paper you can find. Butcher paper is awesome! Draw two vertical lines down the paper to make three columns. Talk to your child about the show you are about to watch together. If it is a show about monkeys, ask your child to tell you everything he or she knows about monkeys. In the first column, make a big k at the top. Under the k, make a list of everything your child knows about monkeys. After you compile the list, ask your child what he or she wants to know about monkeys. Make a big question mark at the top of the middle column. Help your child to make questions using the question words: who, what, where, when, why, and how. Write the questions in the column. Let your child make the question marks. Now, watch the show together. When a question is answered on the show, pause the tape and check it off the list. When the show is over, make a big l in the last column. Make a list of everything your child learned. Now, go back and check the questions. Did they all get answered? If not, go to the computer or the library and find the answer!

CHAPTER 5

The Reading–Writing Relationship: Learning about Reading through Writing Experiences

We began to explore the connection between reading and writing in some of the earlier chapters of this book. I am devoting an entire chapter to writing because it is such an important partner in the development of your child as a communicator and learner.

To get started, it is always a great idea to collect paper. White paper, colored paper, tissue paper, construction paper, note paper, postcards, old letterhead from the office—anything you can get! Buy some bins or containers to help keep things neat. Start collecting Tupperware boxes or shoe boxes to keep pencils, pens, crayons, markers, gel pens, paint pens, stamps, and other cool utensils that can be used for writing. Whenever you have some writing to do, pull out these wonderful tools and have your child join you.

At first, your child will just be pretending. He or she will watch you and want to do what you are doing. Talk about what you are doing when you write. Explain why it is important. For example, you could explain, "I am going to write some thank-you notes to my family because they sent those wonderful gifts to us for Christmas. It is always important to say thank you, but people like to get a note, too. Would you like to make one?" Encourage your child to design his or her own note or card and to tell you about it. Ask questions! "Tell me about what you wrote. Who is in that picture?" If you are going to the supermarket, pull out some coupons and talk about them: "This is a coupon for cereal. We can use it to help us buy corn flakes or corn pops. Which ones should we buy? Let's put that on our list. See, I wrote corn pops right there. Can you help me and make a list, too?" By sharing your purpose for writing and including your child, you will help him or her understand that this form of communication is an important part of our lives.

At first, your child will learn by copying you and others. Encourage him or her to copy letters from words found around the house. Ask your child to write his or her name whenever you can think of a reason. Let your child play with all the paper and materials you have collected. Display his or her efforts on the walls and refrigerator door. Mail them to grandparents with great ceremony. Children love to explore different writing tools, so they may spend an hour just using one stamp, or they may make a great collage by mixing pen, marker, crayon, stamps, and anything else they can get their hands on and putting it all on one piece of paper. Whatever your child does, ask him or her to share and tell you all about it.

Your child will experiment with holding the pencil or crayon in a variety of ways. You may want to demonstrate the correct way to hold a pencil at some point, but it is a good idea to let your child explore on his or her own. Some children have very unique ways of holding their writing utensils, but they get the job done. If you notice that your child is having difficulty or that his or her hand tires quickly, you can give some pointers.

Your child's first efforts will consist of drawings and pictures, wavy scribbles, lines, and even letterlike scribbles. As time progresses, you will recognize random letters and patterned letters in the mix, but there may be little rhyme or reason to your child's choices. The assortment of scribbles, lines, and letters will cover the page in a hodgepodge. This is great. The awareness is growing, but the connection hasn't been made. After a while, you will begin to see patterned letter strings arranged in a column or a row. Now your little one is beginning to understand that letters and words flow in a direction! Eventually, you will see your child's name and letters from his or her name within the patterns. You may also see a few sight words interspersed in the mix.

Small motor development is important in writing. As your child emerges as a writer, it is important to encourage the use of his or her hands in a variety of ways. This helps the small muscles of the hand to develop and builds strength and coordination. There are about thirty-eight effective muscles in the hand. Many of these muscles are used in just a few daily activities. A small child needs to have opportunities to help these muscles become limber and strong. Cutting with scissors, punching holes with a hole puncher, and stringing beads, noodles, or cereal are all great ways to help small motor development. Experimenting with paint is also a fun and creative way to increase your child's agility. Paint with paint brushes, pipe cleaners, feathers, or noodles (cooked or raw). Cut up vegetables and make prints, and let your child's creativity flow. The concept that feelings and ideas can be communicated by putting something down on paper begins to grow in your child. The child has a new outlet to express himself or herself.

Start making books! As you create pictures and works of art, ask your child to tell you the story. Write it on the picture. Collect a few and staple or glue them together into a book. Read the book to your child. Have your child read it back to you. Make a cover. Be sure to let your child write his or her name on the cover. Ask how it feels to be the author of a real book.

Add to your paper and writing collection and expand it into a bookmaking center. Glue sticks, staplers, scissors, blank books, book covers, paper clips, and anything else you have that might makes sense can be put into a bin. When your child creates a book, ask him or her to "read" it to you. Ask your child if he or she would like you to add words on the pages. If your child agrees, be sure to write down exactly what he or she says. Don't be tempted to add words or to correct grammar. Your child needs to understand the idea of dictation. What he or she says is written exactly!

Computers are important writing tools. In this day and age, it is very likely that you have a computer at home. If not, your local library (remember your very good friend over there, the reference librarian?) has computers in the children's section and access to some learning software for your child's exploration. Perhaps grandma and grandpa have a computer at their house and you can go have a wonderful visit. You may have an intense fear or aversion to computers. It's time to get past that! It is a good experience for your child to have some exposure to this wonderful tool. Just the keyboard alone has hundreds of opportunities for learning. I strongly encourage you to look for a way to integrate computer moments into your life.

The keyboard of the computer has our alphabet arranged in a non-alphabetical way. To get accustomed to this arrangement, play a game with your child: "Find the letter *a*. What letter is next to it? Oh, an *s*. What sound does the letter *s* make?" Take some time to practice typing in letters and words. The keyboard provides a lot of opportunity for conversations about the alphabet letters and the sounds they make.

The curious little attachment to the computer that provides the control for the user has a cute little name—the "mouse." The mouse is an excellent tool for practicing eye-hand coordination and manual dexterity. There are many beginning computer programs that help children learn to manipulate a mouse.

There are so many different software products on the market today that it can be confusing to make selections that are age appropriate for a young child. I will make some recommendations, but as the market continues to expand and change, new and better products are being developed and the list may become quickly outdated. I think a visit to your local library is the first step to making good choices. Ask the librarian to show you what is new and popular with children. Ask to try some of them yourself. Check some out. If you find a few activities that your child loves, buy them.

There are also many games and activities that you can experience online. The best thing about these programs is that they are free! Using a search engine, type in a search for children's educational software. There are many Web sites that evaluate and rate children's software, sort of a consumer report of kids' games and activities. Explore!

As I mentioned earlier, technology changes quickly, but a few great programs have been around for a number of years and are still loved by preschoolers:

- *Alphabet Express* by School Zone Interactive. This crazy and zany software has high-quality animation. Kids go aboard the "Alphabet Express" train. The colorful main screen consists of upper- and lowercase letters of the alphabet as an animated train does laps around the letters waiting for your child to click on a letter. Children find that each letter of the alphabet has its very own destination of activities to explore.
- *Kid Pix* by Broderbund. *Kid Pix* is an easy-to-use graphics and writing program. Children can create pictures with captions and

turn them into slide show stories. Print the slide shows and make them into books. This is a wonderful way for children *and* adults to learn to create their first slide show on a computer! That's how I learned.

- *Reader Rabbit* by Broderbund. This is a whole line of learning software. The preschool versions have activities that include matching, sorting, patterns, colors, shapes, letters, and word meanings. There is also a Web site that has some free activities online.
- *Bailey's Book House* by Edmark. This software is a little more advanced. Bailey and his friends invite kids to explore the sounds and meanings of letters, words, rhymes and stories.

ACTIVITIES FOR ENCOURAGING EMERGENT WRITERS

Helping your child to gain the small motor dexterity and coordination needed to be a strong writer is an important task. These simple activities can help to develop the small muscles in the hand and improve coordination, plus providing tactile reinforcement. Children learn visually and auditorily, but they also need hands-on activities and tactile experiences. Tactile experiences help children become familiar with something through touch. Learning the letter shapes is enhanced when they can actually feel the shapes. Most of these activities will seem very simplistic, but they have been successful in engaging a child's interest while building small muscle strength and flexibility.

Tactile Letters. Create letters with different materials: shaving cream, play dough, pipe cleaners, blocks, salt, sand, and pudding.

Name Trace. Print your child's name on a clean, vinyl placemat. At snack time, give your child cereal, raisins, or other finger foods and have him or her cover the name with the snacks. Eat!

Clothes Line. Buy some colorful plastic clothespins or regular old wooden ones. Tie a length of rope between two chairs. Give your child a pile of material scraps, old mittens, gloves, or other small items. Show your child how to hang the clothes. The simple act of operating a clothespin helps to develop the muscles in the hand that are used for writing. Add a song to make it fun.

Nuts and Bolts. Collect an assortment of large nuts and bolts and put them in a bin or shoebox. Your child will have hours of fun just trying to screw them together and take them apart. If you are especially handy, set up a small board and teach your child how to use screws and a screwdriver or to hammer in nails with a small hammer. You can also buy ready-made toys for this purpose.

Tweezers. Collect an assortment of tweezers. Some have rounded tips, others are pointed, and some have handles like tiny scissors. You can also add small ice tongs to the collection. Mix up some small food items of differing colors and shapes: for example, cereal circles, gummy bears, popcorn, or cheese puffs. Take an old, but clean, egg carton and ask your child to sort the items, using the tweezers and tongs to carry out the job.

Lacing Cards. Most toyshops and educational stores have ready-made lace up cards. You can also make your own, using old greeting cards. Just punch holes around the edges of the cards. Cut some twelve-inch pieces of yarn or string and tape the ends. Taping the ends will keep them from fraying and getting caught in the holes. Give the cards and yarn to your child and have him or her practice weaving the yarn into the holes.

Boards and Boards. Keep your eyes open for sales on magnetic boards, wipe-off boards, and chalk boards. Children love to have different kinds of writing opportunities. Colored chalk is always popular. In the beginning, you can write letters on the board and have your child trace them. After awhile, your child be able to do it on his or her own.

Glue Letters. Did you know that you can add paint to regular white glue and make it different colors? Buy some small bottles and mix in a little bit of tempura paint. Make three or four different colors. You can draw some letters on construction paper or tag board and have your child trace them with glue. When the glue dries, your child can run his or her fingers over the letters for a tactile experience!

Carbon Paper. Wow, do they still make that? It may not be easy to find, but it's a great learning tool for kids. They can practice tracing words and pictures onto another piece of paper. Then, they can add an artistic touch by coloring or painting the final product.

As your child starts to write with some consistency and his or her interest in sitting and writing increases, you can begin a more structured approach to writing promotion. In addition to providing lots of materials for writing, you can encourage your young writer in many ways. Here are some ideas to start:

- Questions, questions. Children begin asking a ceaseless string of questions when they begin to speak. Start writing the questions down in a spiral notebook or on a piece of poster board if you have the wall space. Name the book or board something like "Our World of Questions" or "Wonderful Wondering." Each time your child has a question, say: "That is a good question, let's add it to our list." After writing the question, you can answer it, look it up in a book or on the Internet, or even take a trip to the library. It depends upon the question and the time you have to answer it. The essential thing is to recognize every question as important. It is also great modeling to let your child know that you may not know all the answers, but you know where to look or who to ask.
- Secret Messages. Write simple notes to your child and leave them in fun places. If your child goes to preschool, put a note in an envelope and put it in his or her pocket. Write your child's name in big letters on the front. Be sure the message is something he or she can read. "I love you" or "Have a happy day" can be simple phrases that make your child's day. Encourage your child to leave notes for you. Have a big collection of colorful sticky notes in the house. Leave little notes for your child on the bathroom mirror or in his or her toy box. Start with one or two phrases. After you read the note to your child a few times, he or she will begin to recognize familiar phrases.
- Pen Pals. It is never too early to start your child on the road to consistent correspondence. Sometimes it seems that letter writing is a lost art, but children love to get mail. If you have a friend who has a child the same age, you can set up a weekly pen pal time that will make a huge contribution to your child's life as a reader and writer. Just make a commitment to writing once every week or two. Include little notes, stories and pictures. Let your child address the envelope, put on the stamp, and put it in the

mailbox. The excitement of getting mail will fuel his or her love of writing.

- Charts. Charts are visual pictures of facts and data. Reading charts is an important skill. Making charts can help your child to organize thoughts and ideas. Begin with a simple idea and create a chart to hang on the refrigerator. You can buy wipe-off boards that have the days of the week on them. You can keep a log of activities or chores on a weekly basis and review what you did at the end of the week at a glance. Another idea is to make a chart of the number of sight words your child is learning (see figure 5.1).

- TV Reviewers. Television has become an integral part of American family life. Although some families may spend too much time in front of the TV, most people enjoy watching TV for an hour or two a day. Sometimes, it's nice to just watch and listen. Make the most of your child's TV time by keeping track of the shows he or she watches and rate the shows on a scale from one to ten. At the end of the week, look back at the log and decide what was the best show your child watched that week. This exercise only takes a moment, but it will be packed with some interesting learning. First, your child will have an opportunity to express his or her opinion. Second, you'll be able to monitor how much TV your

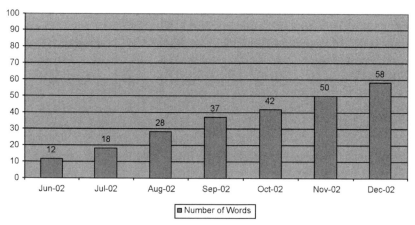

Taylor's Sight Word Growth

Figure 5.1.   *An Example of the Development of a Child's Sight Word Vocabulary over Six Months.*

child is watching. Third, it will help you learn what kinds of shows your child is interested in. Fourth, your child can eventually learn to write names of shows he or she watches regularly and make a rating on paper. Save these in a book, too.

- Recipe Box. If your child enjoys cooking with you, help him or her to make a recipe box. Buy a small plastic file cardholder and some 3 × 5 index cards. Show your child some recipe cards. Let your child copy a few favorite recipes. Ask your child to make up some recipes. Suggest simple things like making a peanut butter sandwich (see figure 5.2).

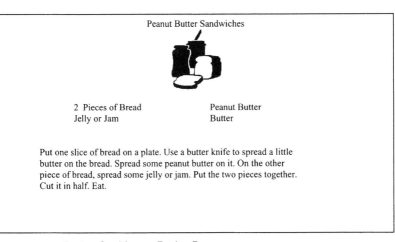

Peanut Butter Sandwiches

2 Pieces of Bread   Peanut Butter
Jelly or Jam   Butter

Put one slice of bread on a plate. Use a butter knife to spread a little butter on the bread. Spread some peanut butter on it. On the other piece of bread, spread some jelly or jam. Put the two pieces together. Cut it in half. Eat.

Figure 5.2.   *Recipe Card from a Recipe Box.*

CHAPTER 6

Building Comprehension Strategies

Reading comprehension can be described as an intricate system of drawing meaning from print. This process requires an understanding of how phonemes, or speech sounds, are connected to print and the ability to decode or sound out unfamiliar words. It also requires the ability to read fluently, adequate background information and vocabulary to foster understanding, active strategies to make a connection from print to meaning, and the motivation to read.

Just because a child has a large sight word vocabulary and can sound out and decode words does not ensure a complete understanding of what he or she is reading. A reader has to be able to make connections to the words while reading them. Reading the words and connecting them to what you know has to be happening simultaneously and continuously while a person is reading.

Earlier chapters explored the development of phonemic awareness and how to foster the development of this important skill. Look for opportunities to help your child see the relationship between sounds and the words that are on the pages of a book. Choose a fun picture book with a repetitive text and colorful pictures, like *Goodnight Moon* by Margaret Wise Brown. I will create an example of how you can use a book to develop phonemic awareness and decoding skills and to activate background knowledge and connections between your child and the story.

I have chosen *Goodnight Moon* by Margaret Wise Brown for many reasons. The pictures are simple and colorful. The story is uncomplicated. There is no central character. It uses simple speech that small children are familiar with and a time of day when children are ready for quiet time. The text has enough repetition for even a very young child to follow the story and remember key words. There are rhyming words that are predictable, so a small child can interact with the text. In addition, it is a very endearing and well-loved piece of children's literature. So, sit down in a comfortable chair and get cozy. Talk to your child about the story before you start. Follow the example below:

"Look at this book. What pictures do you see? I see the fireplace, too. Look at the picture over the fireplace. What do you see? Yes, a cow is jumping over the moon. Remember the song we sing about that? 'Hey diddle, diddle, the cat and the fiddle, the cow jumped over the moon. The little dog laughed to see such sport and the dish ran away with the spoon.' Sing it with me. What else do you see in the picture? I see a window, too. What's in the window? What kind of moon is it? When the moon is round, we call it a full moon. Look at the moon in the painting over the fireplace. That is a crescent moon. The moon looks like a crescent roll!

"Look at the title of the book. What letters do you see? Let's count how many o's there are in the title. There are four. Look how the o's are in pairs. The first pair is in the word *goodnight*. That pair is making the sound that is in the word *wood*. Look at the ones in the word *moon*. They are making a sound like an owl makes or is in the word *who*. Pairs of o's can work together to make two different sounds!

"What do you think this story is going to be about? What do you think about when I say, 'Goodnight'? I think about bedtime, too. Do you think this is going to be a bedtime book? I think that you are right. The moon is out at night and the book is called *Goodnight Moon*, so it will probably be a good bedtime story."

This is an illustration of a way to introduce a new book to a child. Take a few minutes to explore the cover. Spending time before reading a story is an important part of building good reading comprehension strategies. The time you take before reading, to explore what your child already knows about a subject or idea, can help your child to make connections between the story and his or her life.

During the story, stop and ask your child questions. Talk about the words and the pictures. Ask your child what is going to happen next. *Goodnight Moon* has a lot of opportunity for comprehension activation. Each page has a number of objects and toys. Your child will be able to point them out and name them. The entire story takes place in a child's bedroom, so the setting is constant. However, each page adds more objects. This requires activation of memory. You can read the story and leave out the words for each object. Point to the object, and your child is helping you "read" the story.

After you finish, spend some time talking about the story. See how many items your child can remember from the book. Ask your child what he or she says goodnight to before going to bed. Talk about why the little bunny keeps saying "goodnight" to all the things in her room. Discuss how there are times when your child isn't quite ready to fall asleep. What are some of the ways he or she tries to make the moments before bedtime last?

This is a very simple example of three important keys to building good reading comprehension: before, during, and after reading strategies. The object of spending time before reading is to establish a purpose and a plan in the mind of the reader. A young child has a lot of mental activity going on all day long. Taking a few moments to think about the story and what he or she already knows about the subject helps your child to focus. Helping your child to understand the purpose of the story before you begin is a great skill to model. As your child grows as a reader, the ability to set a purpose for reading can make a difference. It is also a great time to practice making predictions about what might happen in the story. Strong readers constantly predict and reinvent ideas as they move through a story.

During reading, take opportunities to continue making predictions, but also find ways to compare and contrast events, ideas, and characters. By asking your child what the little bunny is thinking about in the story, *Goodnight Moon*, you can compare the bunny's bedtime avoidance ideas and strategies to the ones your child uses. While reading, try to help your child visualize the information that is described in the text. The great thing about children's literature is that the wonderful pictures make visualization easy. Take it a little bit farther by asking, "What do you think the little bunny might have in his drawers and closet?" Continue to make comments that help to make connections to situations and events your child is familiar with. This helps to keep your child connected to the story.

It is also important to stop now and then and have your child retell what is happening in the story. Retelling helps to collect and organize facts and ideas while reading. The ability to recall information is an important reading comprehension skill. Retelling is a strategy that builds this ability.

Retelling is also an important part of after reading time. Help your child take time to think about what he or she knew before the reading and what connections and learning were made during the reading. Taking this time after reading helps put things together and begins the work of remembering the information.

Children's literature is fun. It doesn't take a long time to read a children's book. But, if you add the before, during, and after strategies, you will find that it can take at least fifteen minutes longer to read a book. Take the time. Building a strong foundation of good reading strategies will help you raise a strong and effective reader.

It is also a good idea to be aware of the basic structure of children's books. Most stories have a setting, main characters, a basic plot, a goal, a problem, and a solution. The setting in the traditional story of *Little Red Riding Hood* is the woods and grandmother's house. Little Red Riding Hood and the wolf are the main characters. Little Red Riding Hood's goal is to bring her basket of goodies to her sick grandmother. The wolf's goal is to eat the goodies and Little Red Riding Hood. That's where the problem occurs! The plot is the events that happen from the beginning of the story to its conclusion. The solution happens when the main character's goal is attained.

Although this was a quickie version of story structure, it helps to be aware that most stories can be explained using these elements. I am not suggesting that you teach these concepts to a preschooler! However, I think it is important to be aware of the structure and talk to your child about these things in a simpler way.

"Where does Little Red Riding Hood live? What is she going to do? Why does the wolf follow her? What does he want? Why is Little Red Riding Hood going through the woods? Why does she talk to the wolf? Is the wolf a friend or a stranger? Is it a good idea to talk to strangers? What do you think is in the basket? What happened to grandma? What is Little Red Riding Hood's problem? How is her problem solved? What else could have happened at the end?"

You can ask questions during and after reading to help create an idea of story structure in your child's mind. As your child begins to think about stories in this way, it is easier for him or her to recall facts and events from reading. You can also use the story elements to guide your child's writing. Familiarity with story structure makes better writers, too.

Summarizing is another excellent comprehension strategy that you can help your child build. The ability to summarize is being able to condense the story and give the main ideas. Similar to retelling, summarizing is retelling a story in a shortened form. When children begin to read for academic purposes, summarizing is a very important skill. Many children have difficulty breaking down a large reading selection and briefly retelling it by just hitting the key concepts and main ideas. If you begin to practice this skill at a young age, you will give your child an advantage. Summarizing uses the higher level thinking skills of application and evaluation of knowledge.

Vocabulary is also an important part of developing good reading comprehension strategies. The best way to build a good vocabulary is to read. The more you read to and with your child, the more words he or she will be exposed to. Another way is to have a conversation and take time to explain words that your child doesn't know. Encourage your child to ask what an unknown word is or what it means. Model this behavior by asking other adults about words.

I have a wonderful friend who is an excellent model. We enjoy meeting at a coffee shop and reading books together. From time to time, he will stop and say, "Do you know what this word means? It is used in this sentence." And he will proceed to read the sentence to me. If I know what the word means, we'll talk it over. If I don't, I look it up. We have a great friendship, and we have both learned from each other. You can do the same with your child. If you are reading a book to your child and you are unsure of a word, grab a dictionary and look it up.

Encourage discussion of new words. If you look up a word, make an effort to use it throughout the day. If your child learns a new word, encourage him or her to use it in a few sentences. If you hear the word on TV or see it in a magazine, let your child know. "Hey, look. Remember when we were reading yesterday and we learned that new word? Well, there it is!"

If your child asks you what a word means while you are reading, stop and talk about it. Read the entire sentence. Ask your child what he or she thinks the word means based on the rest of the sentence. See if the pictures on the page give a clue. This is the strategy of using context clues to understand unknown words. You can do this when your child is reading and cannot recognize or sound out a word, too.

Reading is more than just knowing letters and sounds. It is engaging and connecting your life and your experiences to the written word. It is a relationship. Relationships take nurturing and effort to grow. Reading comprehension takes time. It takes experiences. The best way to build great strategies is to read, but you can do more. You can use before, during, and after strategies to build better reading awareness in your child. You can help your child learn to retell and summarize. You can help him or her to develop a strong vocabulary. All of these things will make your child more than a reader; your child will be a strong and effective reader.

Comprehension games can reinforce the strategies you are building when you read to and with your child. I have a few ideas to share. You may find more in educational stores.

Retelling Skill Builder. Go to garage sales and library book sales. You can pick up children's books for a small amount of money. Choose a familiar book or one with a simple plot. Cut out the pages. Lay them on the floor out of order. Read the pages with your child and try to put the book back together in the right order.

Missing Word. Use small sticky notes to cover the last word of each phrase in a rhyming story. Read the story and have your child guess the covered word.

I Spy. There are some wonderful *I Spy* books on the market. *Where's Waldo* is another type of look-and-find book. The *I Spy* books have a number of objects on a page. The goal is for children to find different things on the page. This requires the skills of skimming and scanning. We use these skills every day when we read. We are looking for specific pieces of information. Using these books can develop the skills needed for this reading strategy.

Words and Pictures. Use family pictures to create a great comprehension game. Choose four or five family pictures. On an index card, write a short sentence about what is happening in the picture. Lay the photos out. Read a card to your child, or let him or her read it, and match the card to the right picture.

Question Box. Get a medium-sized square box. Tape it closed. On the sides, top, and bottom write a question word: who, what, where, when, why, or how (see figure 6.1). Read a story together. Toss the box to your child. Ask your child to read the word that is on the top. Ask him or her to answer the question.

Story maps and graphic organizers are tools that teachers use to help children understand the structure and content of a story. A story map

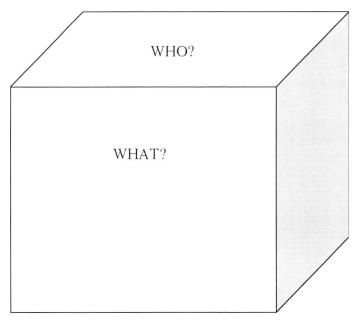

Figure 6.1.   *Question Box.*

draws the basic story elements on a chart so children can see a picture of the main content of the story. Graphic organizers arrange thoughts in a visual way. As your child begins to read on his or her own, you can try using these tools to reinforce good comprehension strategies. Following are examples of a few simple story maps and graphic organizers to try.

The KWL is a well-known and well-used tool in education today. It is a very simple concept that has wonderful results. Use a piece of paper, wipe-off board, or chalkboard to make a three-column graph. At the top of the first column, make a capital *k*. The letter *k* stands for the word *know*. In this column, you write everything you know about a concept before you read about it. In the middle column, write a capital *w*. The letter *w* stands for the word *wonder*, or the question, "What do I want to know?" In this column, you will create questions. Ask yourself, what do you want to know about that subject? Generate who, what, where, when, why, and how questions. Fill in the *k* and *w* columns before you begin reading. In the last column, write a capital *l*. The letter *l* stands for the word *learn*. In this column, you will write down everything you have learned by reading the selection. This step is done during and after reading.

The KWL can be done before, during, and after reading and many other activities. It is a wonderful tool to use when going on family outings like a trip to the zoo or museum. "What do we already know about the zoo? What do we want to know about?" After the trip, write about what you learned on your excursion.

Imagine that you were going to read a story about an elephant. Talk about what you know about elephants and write it down in the *k* column. Then, talk about what you want to know and write questions in the *w* column. After you read, write down everything you learned (see figure 6.2).

Venn diagrams are great tools to help children compare and contrast information. You can use one to compare two characters or two stories. Comparing two versions of a fairy tale can be fun. There is a wonderful version of the story of *The Three Little Pigs* written by Jon Scieszka called *The True Story of the Three Little Pigs by A. Wolf*. In this story, the wolf is the narrator. He explains that he never intended to hurt the pigs; he was just trying to make a cake for his sick grandmother. He happened to have a bad cold, which caused him to sneeze a lot. When

K What Do I Know?	W What Do I Want to Know?	L What Have I learned?

Elephants are big.
Elephants have trunks.
Elephants can come
  from Africa,
Asia, or India.
Some elephants have tusks.
Elephants have thick,
  wrinkly skin.
Elephants are supposed to
  like peanuts.
	Why do elephants have
	  trunks?
	How big can elephants get?
	What do elephants eat?
	Where do elephants like
	  to sleep?
	How long can an
	  elephant live?
	Why do some elephants
	  have tusks?	

Figure 6.2. *An Example of the KWL Reading Strategy.*

he sneezed, the pigs' houses just happened to fall down. He never tried to do it! Read this to your child and talk about how it is different from the traditional story. Make notes on a Venn diagram to see the differences (see figure 6.3).

The Traditional Story of the *Three Little Pigs*   *The True Story of the Three Little Pigs by A. Wolf*

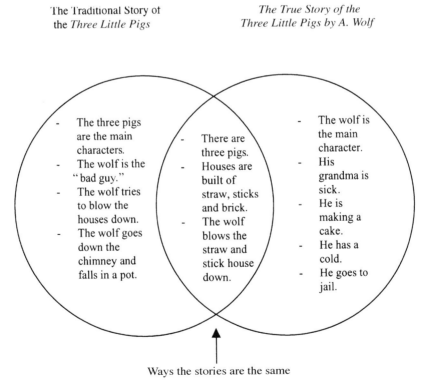

Ways the stories are the same

Figure 6.3. *An Example of a Venn Diagram.*

A simple story map is a one-page, quick way to see a story at a glance. Fill in the section for each story element. You can have your child draw pictures to explain the beginning, middle, and end of the story (see figure 6.4).

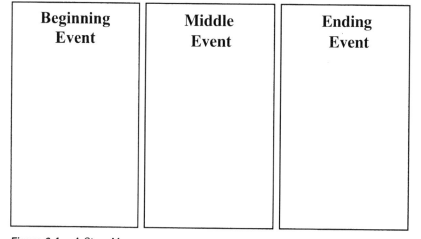

Figure 6.4.   *A Story Map.*

CHAPTER 7

How to Assess the Progress: Five Basic Assessment Tools to Monitor Your Child's Reading Development

It is always a great idea to monitor the progress of your child. It is helpful to have a few simple and easy-to-use tools. The most basic early skills a reader develops are phonemic awareness and a sight word vocabulary. As your child learns to read, he or she will develop basic knowledge of letter sounds and how to blend the sounds. You can monitor your child's readiness to read by identifying the concepts about print he or she knows and needs to know. All of these assessments are for one purpose: to learn what your child knows and what he or she still needs to learn. Use the information to help you guide your child's reading development.

Phonemic awareness is the ability to hear and recognize sounds. It is also the knowledge that sounds make words and that individual sounds are used to create words. You can do some informal, preliminary checking to see if your child can identify the beginning and ending sounds he or she hears in words. Tell your child that you are going to say some words, and you want him or her to tell you the first sound he or she hears when you say the word. If your child can do this, try again with end sounds. Explain that this time, you want him or her to listen for the sound the word ends with. If your child is able to isolate the first sound and last sound, he or she is successfully developing phonemic awareness (see figure 7.1).

Sight words are words that have been memorized. Remember research indicates that when a child sees a word two hundred times, it becomes part of his or her sight word vocabulary. It takes a while for children to build an extensive sight vocabulary. A goal may be to know the

Date: _____

Directions: Tell your child: "I am going to say all the sounds I hear in a word. I won't say the word, just the sounds that make up the word. While I am saying them, put the sounds together in your head. I want you to tell me the word that you hear when you put these sounds together. You say it fast. Let me show you."

Model: You may need to do this a few times. Try not to use words on the assessment. "If I say /c/ /a/ /t/ the word is . . . *cat.*"

Do it together: "Now let's try one together. Say it fast. If I say /p/ /a/ /t/, what word do you say? Yes, the word is . . . *pat.*"

The assessment: "Listen to the sounds and tell me the word those sounds make." Say each sound and make a slight pause.

The Word	The Sounds	Your Child's Response
bat	/b/ /a/ /t/	_____
bed	/b/ /e/ /d/	_____
dog	/d/ /o/ /g/	_____
big	/b/ /i/ /g/	_____
hug	/h/ /u/ /g/	_____
fan	/f/ /a/ /n/	_____
men	/m/ /e/ /n/	_____
pot	/p/ /o/ /t/	_____
run	/r/ /u/ /n/	_____

The purpose of the assessment is to see if your child can hear the sounds and blend them to make a word. If your child is not ready, wait and try it in a few months.

Figure 7.1.   *Phonemic Awareness Assessment.*

first one hundred words by the beginning of first grade. However, if your child is not ready, don't push. Start with just a few words and build (see figure 7.2).

Phonics knowledge is understanding the relationship between written letters and spoken sounds. Knowing the names of the letters of the alphabet is the first step (see figure 7.3). After that is mastered, you can help your child learn the sounds. Keeping track of what letters your child does and does not know can be helpful (see figure 7.4).

Concepts about print is a strategy developed by Marie M. Clay, a teacher and researcher who has written a great deal about reading development. Concepts about print knowledge is knowing how books are structured and how they are read. Children with this knowledge have the basic skills needed to begin reading.

There are beginning elements that an emergent reader is learning, and being aware of your child's knowledge of these concepts is helpful. Your

You can make flash cards or use Microsoft PowerPoint to make a slide show. Type in one word for each slide. If you make flash cards, use 3 × 5 index cards. Print neatly and make the words big and easy to read. Turn over one card at a time. If your child recognizes it, put it in one pile. If not, place it in another pile. After you go through all the words, show the ones your child did not recognize a second time. Circle the words he or she knows on an assessment record like this one. Date the sheet and save it. This will help you keep track of the words your child learns and retains. Do a check every few months to monitor his or her growth.

a	by	he	make	see	very
about	came	her	many	she	was
after	can	here	me	so	we
again	come	him	much	some	went
all	did	his	my	take	were
am	do	how	new	that	what
an	down	I	no	the	when
and	eat	if	not	their	where
any	for	in	of	them	which
are	four	into	old	then	who
as	get	is	on	there	will
at	give	it	one	they	with
be	go	just	or	this	work
been	good	know	our	three	you
before	had	like	out	to	your
big	has	little	put	two	
but	have	long	said	up	

Figure 7.2. *First Hundred Sight Words Assessment.*

child is learning that print carries a meaning and message. There is a one-to-one correspondence between words read and those printed in the text. There are conventions of print such as directionality (left to right, top to bottom), differences between letters and words, distinctions between upper and lowercase, and punctuation. Books have some common characteristics such as author, title, front, back, and so on. All of these elements are foundations of reading books. By using the concepts outlined in the assessment and asking the questions that accompany it, you can begin to learn about your child's reading development (see figures 7.5 and 7.6).

An important note about assessing your child: you do not have to formally use any of these assessments. You can use the ideas expressed in them, even when your child is very young. As he or she begins to show readiness to start reading, you can use the assessments to monitor your child's progress. It is really important to use these assessments in as natural a way as possible. If your child is aware that you are writing things down or feels pressure, it may affect his or her feeling about reading. Pick a few ideas from an assessment. Ask questions and watch your child's responses. Make notes about his or her answers and reactions later. This is information for you to use to help your child grow as a reader.

Use flashcards or alphabet manipulative letters with your child to complete this assessment. Hold up one letter at a time. Ask your child to name the letter. Do this assessment with capital letters first, then lowercase. Your child may know all the capitals, but not all the lowercase letters. This assessment will help you determine what to work on. Check again in a few months.

A	_____	a	_____
B	_____	b	_____
C	_____	c	_____
D	_____	d	_____
E	_____	e	_____
F	_____	f	_____
G	_____	g	_____
H	_____	h	_____
I	_____	i	_____
J	_____	j	_____
K	_____	k	_____
L	_____	l	_____
M	_____	m	_____
N	_____	n	_____
O	_____	o	_____
P	_____	p	_____
Q	_____	q	_____
R	_____	r	_____
S	_____	s	_____
T	_____	t	_____
U	_____	u	_____
V	_____	v	_____
W	_____	w	_____
X	_____	x	_____
Y	_____	y	_____
Z	_____	z	_____

Date: _____

Figure 7.3.   *Alphabet Letter Identification Assessment.*

In this assessment, you will hold up an alphabet letter and ask your child what sound it makes. If a letter makes more than one sound, as in vowels, ask what short /a/ says and what long /a/ says. In the case of consonants with two sounds, ask what soft /c/ says and what hard /c/ says.

A	_____ long		_____ short	
B	_____			
C	_____		_____ hard	
D	_____			
E	_____ long		_____ short	
F	_____			
G	_____ soft		_____ hard	
H	_____			
I	_____ long		_____ short	
J	_____			
K	_____			
L	_____			
M	_____			
N	_____			
O	_____ long		_____ short	
P	_____			
Q	_____			
R	_____			
S	_____ soft		_____ hard	
T	_____			
U	_____ long		_____ short	
V	_____			
W	_____			
X	_____			
Y	_____			
Z	_____			

Date: _____

Figure 7.4. *Letter–Sound Awareness Assessment.*

These questions accompany the "Your Child's Print Knowledge" assessment. Look over the questions first. Practice some of these concepts with your child for a few weeks before actually going through all the assessment steps. Check and see what he or she already knows. Use this knowledge to guide your reading time with your child. For example, if your child is having a hard time tracking from left to right, model with your finger or a pointer while you read, so he or she understands the direction your eyes move along the page.

1. Hand your child the book. Ask: "Where is the cover?"
2. Ask your child to "read" to you. Even if they are not yet reading, see if they follow the book from beginning to end.
3. Ask: "Can you point to the words? Can you point to the pictures?"
4. Ask: "Can you point to a letter?"
5. Ask: "Can you point to a word?"
6. Ask: "Where is the beginning of the book?"
7. Ask your child to "read" to you. Even if your child is not yet reading, see if he or she can follow the words on the page from left to right.
8. Ask: "Can you point to a. . . . (a, b, c, and so on)."
9. Point to the capital letters on the pages of the book. Ask your child to name them. Use the alphabet letter name assessment to see which letters your child knows.
10. Point to the lowercase letters on the pages of the book. Ask your child to name them. Use the alphabet letter name assessment to see which letters your child knows.

Figure 7.5. *Questions for the "Your Child's Print Knowledge" Assessment.*

These concepts are important for emergent readers. By identifying what your child knows and what he or she needs to learn, you can discover areas to focus on when you are reading with your child. If your child is not ready, don't push. Just talk about these concepts while you read. Your child will learn when he or she is ready.

Date: _____

Your Child's Print Knowledge
Using a children's book, explore some questions with your child.

1. My child can show me where/what the cover of the book is.   ☐
2. My child knows to read from front to back.   ☐
3. My child can show me the difference between text and pictures.   ☐
4. My child knows what a letter is.   ☐
5. My child knows what a word is.   ☐
6. My child knows where to begin reading.   ☐
7. My child knows how to read from left to right.   ☐
8. My child can point to letters when I name them.   ☐
9. My child can name the capital letters of the alphabet.   ☐
10. My child can name the lowercase letters of the alphabet.   ☐

Figure 7.6. *Your Child's Print Knowledge Assessment.*

CHAPTER 8

Continuous Progress: Strategies to Ensure Continued Reading Success

The majority of this book focuses on building the foundations of reading readiness. By exploring the ideas shared in the earlier chapters, you will find a variety of activities and resources that will help you in the role you play as your child's first teacher. By the time your child is four or five, you may be considering enrollment in a playgroup or preschool. These opportunities will provide further stimulation of your child's imagination and development.

This last chapter explores some resources that you can use after your child has become a reader.

RESEARCH ABOUT EARLY READING PREPARATION AND READINESS

The information shared below is from data collected by the Early Childhood Longitudinal Study. This study was sponsored by the U.S. Department of Education and The National Center for Education Statistics. The purpose of this study was to assess children's reading skills as they entered kindergarten. Researchers studied children in the fall of 1998, kindergarten in the spring of 1999, and first grade in spring 2000. Sixty-seven percent had letter recognition skills; this increased to 95 percent of children in the spring of their kindergarten year, and 100 percent by the spring of their first-grade year.

SUPPORT FOR HELPING YOUR CHILD
LEARN ALPHABET LETTERS

Children who could recognize their letters and name them before starting kindergarten made greater learning strides in the area of reading development by the end of their first-grade year. This ability is very important for early learners. All the time and energy you spend talking and reading about the alphabet, playing games, and singing songs about the alphabet, as well as all the money you invest in materials and manipulatives you use when your child experiences the alphabet, will pay off. Here are some statistics:

- 99 percent understood the letter–sound relationship at the beginning of words, compared to 95 percent of children who did not have letter recognition skills at the start of kindergarten
- 98 percent understood the letter–sound relationship at the ending of words, compared to 87 percent of children who did not have letter recognition skills at the start of kindergarten
- 92 percent had sight word recognition skills, compared to 63 percent who did not have letter recognition skills at the start of kindergarten
- 60 percent understood words in context, compared to 21 percent who did not have letter recognition skills at the start of kindergarten

Researchers in the Early Childhood Longitudinal Study discovered that by the spring of kindergarten, children should be able to recognize the letters of the alphabet "quickly and effortlessly," and understand the letter–sound relationship at the beginning and end of words. By the spring of first grade, most children should be recognizing words by sight and comprehending words in the context of simple sentences (Denton 2002).

SUPPORT FOR HELPING YOUR CHILD
LEARN PHONEMIC (SOUND) AWARENESS

Children who could understand the letter–sound relationship at the beginning and end of words before starting kindergarten made greater learning strides in the area of reading development by the end of their first-grade year. Helping your child become aware of the sounds in words does not have to be formal. Just use the strategies suggested in this book and take opportunities to talk about sounds. Casually making sound awareness part of everyday interactions with your child will help him or her acquire this crucial skill. Here are some statistics:

- 31 percent could understand the letter–sound relationship at the beginning of words; this increased to 74 percent of children in the spring of their kindergarten year, and 98 percent by the spring of their first-grade year
- 18 percent could understand the letter–sound relationship at the end of words; this increased to 54 percent of children in the spring of their kindergarten year, and 94 percent by the spring of their first-grade year

A good grasp of letter–sound relationships is a basic part of phonemic awareness. You can see that this is important and that most children have not developed a strong understanding of this concept by the beginning of kindergarten.

SUPPORT FOR HELPING YOUR CHILD DEVELOP A SIGHT WORD INVENTORY

Children who had some experiences and exposure to the one hundred basic sight words before starting kindergarten made greater learning strides in the area of reading development by the end of their first-grade year. Here are some statistics:

- 3 percent had sight word recognition skills; skills increased to 14 percent of children in the spring of their kindergarten year, and 83 percent by the spring of their first-grade year
- 1 percent could understand words in context; skills increased to 4 percent of children in the spring of their kindergarten year, and 48 percent by the spring of their first-grade year

Knowing all one hundred sight words before the beginning of kindergarten is unusual, according to this study. As you can see, only 3 percent of the children in the study had sight word recognition skills. Realize that your child may not be ready to master a sight word inventory, but you can expose him or her to many of the words. Remember, a child needs to see a word at least two hundred times for it to become a sight word.

WHAT IS A PHONEME? TIPS FOR
TEACHING PHONEMIC AWARENESS

Phonemes are the smallest units of speech. They are the basic building blocks of speaking, reading, and writing. It isn't necessary for you to become a linguist and know all the ins and outs of the structure of our language, but here are the basics:

- There are twenty-six letters in our alphabet. Five are considered to be vowels. Twenty are consonants. The letter *y* moves back and forth. It is often referred to "and sometimes *y*."
- The five vowels, /a/, /e/, /i/, /o/, and /u/ each make a long and a short sound. Each sound is a phoneme. So, the five vowels make ten phonemes.
- Examples of words with short vowels:

  /a/ cat
  /e/ bet
  /i/ sit
  /o/ pot
  /u/ hut

- Examples of words with long vowels:

  /a/ mate
  /e/ meet
  /i/ kite
  /o/ boat
  /u/ tune

- The twenty-one consonants, counting *y* in the group, make a total of twenty-six sounds, but some are repetitive. Two of the sounds that the letter *y* makes are vowel sounds. The letters *c*, *g*, and *s* make a soft sound and a hard sound, but three of them are the sounds of other consonants. So, the twenty-one consonants make twenty-one sounds and mimic other phonemes.

• The letter *y* can make three phonetic sounds:

A consonant sound: yet
The long /e/ sound: baby
The long /i/ sound: fly d

• There are three consonants that can make two sounds. These are the letters *c*, *g*, and *s*. They can make a soft sound or a hard sound.

	Soft Sounds	Hard Sounds
c	cent (sounds like an /s/)	catch (sounds like a /c/or /k/)
g	gentle (sounds like a /j/)	grab (sounds like a /g/)
s	snake (sounds like an /s/)	hose (sounds like a /z/)

Vowel pairs are two vowels that combine to make one sound. For example, in the word *rain*, you hear three sounds: /r/, long /a/ and /n/. However, there are four letters. The letters *a* and *i* pair up and make one long vowel sound. Consonant blends are two or more consonants that work together to make one sound or phoneme. For example, the word *glad* is made of three phonemes /gl/, short /a/ and /d/. Digraphs are pairs of letters that make one speech sound. Examples of digraphs are /wh/, /ch/, /th/, /sh/, /ph/ and /ng/.

TIPS FOR TEACHING PHONEMIC AWARENESS

All of this information about phonemes may be helpful or confusing. Don't worry. If you get the general idea, you can help your child develop phonemic awareness.

• When you are teaching phonemic awareness, the focus should be on the sounds of words, not on letters or spellings.
• Model specific sounds, such as /s/ in the word *sat*. Ask your child to name the beginning sound in many different words that start with /s/. Practice.
• Begin with short, simple words. Listen for initial /s/ in *sat*, *sit*, *sip*, and *sad* or for long /e/ in *me*, *see*, and *bee*.

- Teach the child to blend phonemes into words. Begin by identifying just one phoneme. Begin by saying: "What sound do you hear first when I say the word *pat*? What sound do you hear first when I say the word *mat*?" Continue working gradually toward blending all the phonemes in the words. "What sounds do you hear when I say the word *pat*? How many sounds do you hear? Let's count them."
- Teach your child to identify the separate phonemes within words. Say: "What is the first sound of *mop*? What is the last sound of *hat*?" Beginning phonemes are easier to identify than final phonemes.
- Once your child is comfortable listening for individual phonemes, teach him or her to break up words into component sounds: "Let's listen for the sounds in the word *baby*. Can you hear them? /b/ /a/ /b/ /y/."

A PHONICS INVENTORY

This is a little more advanced than the inventories in chapter 7. Use this when children are reading some words on their own (see figures 8.1 and 8.2).

- *Alphabet Letter Names.* Ask: "What are the names of these letters?" Point to each of the letters on the child assessment sheet and ask the question. Circle the letters your child does not know. This inventory mixes up the letters. It is a lot easier for a child to name the letters if they are in order.
- *Consonant Sounds.* Ask: "What sound does this letter make?" Point to each of the letters on the child assessment sheet and ask the question. Circle the letters your child does not know. This time, the letters are out of order. You get a clearer idea of your child's knowledge of the sounds.
- *Consonant Digraphs.* (A digraph is a pair of letters that represent a single speech sound, such as the /ph/ in *phone* or the /wh/ in *what*.) Ask: "What sound do these letters make together?" Point to each of the diagraphs on the child assessment sheet and ask the question. Circle the digraphs your child does not know.

Alphabet Letter Names

Q	X	W	K	V	Y	G	H	U	N	O	J	C
D	S	A	I	B	F	E	T	P	M	R	Z	L
I	a	k	s	j	d	h	f	g	t	y	r	u
e	i	w	o	q	p	z	m	c	n	x	b	v

Consonant Sounds

m	l	p	j	n	b	h	y	t	g	v	c	f
d	r	w	s	x	z	q	k					

Consonant Digraphs

wh   ph   th   ch   sh   ng

Consonant Blends

bl   br   sl   sr   cr   cl   pl   pr   gl   gr   dr   sp   fr   fl   tr   str   scr

Vowel Names

a   e   i   o   u

Vowel Sounds

	Short Vowel Sounds	Long Vowel Sounds
	/a/ nap, hat	/a/ cape, ate
	e/ bed, egg	/e/ bead, sleep
	/i/ big, ti	/i/ kite, ripe
	/o/ lot, pot	/o/ boat, cone
	/u/ hug, hut	/u/ tune, flute

Made-Up Words

weg   rif   tas   pob   sug   dav   gim   heb   lom   vub

Reversals

on   lap   was   ten   rat   top   saw   no   pot   net   tar   pal

Figure 8.1. Phonics Inventory Record Sheet.

- *Consonant Blends.* (Consonant blends are two or more consonants that combine to make one sound such as /gl/ in *glad*. The /g/ and the /l/ combine to make a blended sound.) Ask: "What sound do these letters make together?" Point to each of the consonant blends on the child assessment sheet and ask the question. Circle the consonant blends your child does not know.
- *Vowel Names.* Do not show the letters to your child. Ask: "Can you tell me the names of the letters that make the vowel sounds?" or "What are the five vowels?"

Alphabet Letter Names												
Q	X	W	K	V	Y	G	H	U	N	O	J	C
D	S	A	I	B	F	E	T	P	M	R	Z	L
I	a	k	s	j	d	h	f	g	t	y	r	u
e	i	w	o	q	p	z	m	c	n	x	b	v

Consonant Sounds

m	l	p	j	n	b	h	y	t	g	v	c	f
d	r	w	s	x	z	q	k					

Consonant Digraphs

wh	ph	th	ch	sh	ng

Consonant Blends

bl	br	sl	sr	cr	cl	pl	pr	gl
gr	dr	sp	fr	fl	tr	str	scr	

Vowel Names

Listening Section

Vowel Sounds

Listening Section

Made-Up Words

weg	rif	tas	pob	sug
dav	gim	heb	lom	vub

Reversals

on	lap	was	ten	rat	top	saw
no	pot	net	tar	pal		

Figure 8.2. *The Phonics Inventory, Child's Form.*

- *Vowel Sounds.* Do not show the letters to your child. Say: "Listen carefully to the words I say to you. Tell me the vowel you hear in each word."
- *Made-Up Words: Short Vowels.* Say: "These are make-believe words. Read each of these words using a short vowel sound."
- *Reversals.* Say: "Read these words as quickly as you can."

SIGHT WORDS LISTS

Following are the one hundred most frequently used words in the English language sorted by vowel sounds (see figure 8.3). Figure 8.4 is another sight word list showing words in groups of fifty.

Short /a/	Short /e/	Short /i/	Short /o/	Short /u/
an	them	did	not	but
and	then	him	on	just
as	when	if		up
at		his		
can		in		
had		into		
than		is		
that		it		
after		its		
has		which		
		little		
		this		
		will		
		with		

Long /a/	Long /e/	Long /i/	Long /o/	/ou/
make	see	by	most	about
made	each	my	know	out
		find		down
		like		how
		time		now

Long /e/ ending	/th/	Words to Memorize:		
be	the	a	may	two
he	their	all	more	use
we	there	are	no	very
she	these	been	of	was
	they	called	one	water
		could	only	way
		do	or	were
		first	other	what
		for	over	where
		from	people	who
		have	said	words
		her	so	would
		I	some	you
		long	to	your
		many		

Figure 8.3.   *First One Hundred Sight Word Sound List.*

STAGES OF READING: BOOK AND READER ATTRIBUTES AND BOOK IDEAS

The following show stages of child development in reading as well as other aspects of life (see tables 8.1 and 8.2).

My First Sight Words List

a	am	and
at	away	be
big	blue	can
come	do	down
find	for	go
he	help	here
I	in	into
is	it	little
look	make	me
my	no	not
on	one	out
play	ran	red
run	said	see
ten	the	two
three	to	up
we	where	yellow
yes	you	

My Second Sight Word List

all	an	are
as	ate	black
brown	but	by
came	did	eat
four	get	good
had	has	have
his	let	like
must	new	now
of	our`	please
pretty	ride	saw
say	she	so
soon	that	there
they	this	too
under	want	was
well	went	were
what	white	who
will	with	

My Third Sight Word List

after	again	around
ask	because	before
best	could	does
don't	every	first
five	fly	from
give	going	her
him	how	jump
just	know	live

Figure 8.4. First Two Hundred Sight Words in Groups of Fifty Words (Slightly Different List of Words from List of One Hundred Sight Words).

made	many	may
old	once	open
over	put	read
round	sit	some
stop	take	thank
them	then	these
think	those	very
walk	warm	when
which	why	

My Fourth Sight Word List

about	any	been
better	both	bring
call	carry	cold
cut	done	draw
eight	fall	fast
found	full	gave
got	green	grow
hold	hot	hurt
if	its	keep
kind	long	much
myself	off	only
or	own	right
seven	sing	six
sleep	small	start
their	today	together
try	use	work
write	your	

Figure 8.4.   *continued.*

KINDERGARTEN SCREENING

Most states have some kind of prescreening process for children before they enter kindergarten. Many screenings evaluate the development of a child in a variety of areas.

Fine Motor Development: A child's ability to use small muscles to manipulate things. Children with strong fine motor development have success with tasks such as drawing and cutting.

Gross Motor Development: A child's ability to use the muscles of the body with control and to do large muscle tasks such as running and jumping.

Receptive and Expressive Language: Receptive language is a child's understanding of spoken language. Expression is the child's oral communication of ideas and concepts.

Table 8.1. Stages of Reading: Book and Reader Attributes and Book Ideas.

Stage of Reading Readiness	Attributes of Readers at this Stage	Choosing Books that are:	Book Ideas
Pre-emergent (ages 2–3)	Learning the basics of sound through rhyme, rhythm, repetition and natural language. Learning print moves from left to right. Books flow from front to back. Aware that letters have names and sounds. Aware that words are made up of sounds. Memorized chants, rhymes and songs.	Short and have few or no words on a page In large print Repetitious Made up of word patterns and rhyme Full of colorful pictures that provide cues for text Fun, interesting and predictable Familiar, filled with objects or actions in content	Brown Bear, Brown Bear by Bill Martin Jr. Have You Seen My Cat? by Eric Carle Rain by Robert Kalan Footprints in the Snow by Cynthia Benjamin Noise by Joy Cowley
Emergent (ages 4–5)	Building decoding skills as well as a sight vocabulary. Using clues to read words not yet known. Using knowledge of letter–sound relationships, words, and parts of words to check on reading. Self-correcting and cross-checking one source of information against another. Having a bank of a minimum of twenty-five known high-frequency words.	Patterned and short Large print Multiple lines per page Pictures that provide rich prompts for text Sometimes rhyme Written in complete sentences Highly interesting and entertaining Simple concepts and high degree of predictability	Over in the Meadow by Paul Galdone Hattie & the Fox by Mem Fox Time for Bed by Jane Dyer Big Red Barn by Margaret Wise Brown Old Black Fly by Jim Aylesworth

| Ready to Read (ages 5+) | Learning strategies for decoding understanding.
Building fluency and confidence.
Relies less on pictures/patterns and more on text and context.
Having a bank of a minimum of one hundred known high-frequency words.
Writes thought and ideas in a way that is readable (not conventional writing but understandable). | Have more pages (32–48)
Still have large print
More words and sentences per page
Fewer patterns in text
May have short chapters
Pictures throughout
Contain familiar words
Introduce new vocabulary in easy to learn ways
Text is highly interesting and entertaining
Easy to follow structure in nonfiction text | *Frog & Toad Are Friends* by Arnold Lobel
Arthur's Loose Tooth by Lillian Hoban
The Wonderful Pigs of Jillian Jiggs by Phoebe Gilman
Where the Wild Things Are by Maurice Sendak
The Giving Tree by Shel Silverstein |

Table 8.2. Developmental Characteristics of a Child.

Age	Physical Development	Social Development	Emotional Development	Intellectual Development	Development as a Reader
Two years	Walks with stability Runs Goes up and down stairs independently Learning toilet training Uses spoon and fork Can turn pages in a book	Developing a sense of personal identity and independence Self-centered Possessive and demanding Often negative (no!), easily frustrated Resistant to change Responsive to humor Resistant to discipline or reason	Plays alone Sometimes has difficulty sharing Refers to self by name Little concept of others as people Beginning to respond to simple directions	Says words, phrases, and simple sentences Knows up to 275 words Understands simple directions Likes to look at books Short attention span	Plays with books as toys (doesn't yet understand that they contain stories) Enjoys listening to books and stories Not aware that the pages contain words that correspond to a story Attracted to the bright colors and illustrations but doesn't understand that the pictures depict a story Identifies with pictures but not words or letters on the pages

Age	Physical	Social	Emotional	Language	Cognitive
Three Years	Runs with control Marches and stands on one foot Rides tricycle Feeds self well Puts on shoes/stockings Uses buttons Beginning to handle writing utensils	Enjoys being with others Takes turns Knows their gender Enjoys brief group activities	Easy going More secure Greater sense of personal identity Beginning to be adventuresome Enjoys music	Says short sentences Knows nearly 900 words Communicates thoughts, ideas, and needs Tells simple stories Uses words to share thoughts Answers questions Sings songs Recites rhymes	Memorizes books and tries to read them again and again Can tell a story by using illustrations Can recall some characters and events from stories Displays phonemic awareness
Four Years	Hop and jump Cut with scissors Run quickly and with purpose Throw a ball with relative accuracy Small motor muscles developing Increased hand-eye coordination Prints simple letters	Highly social age Enjoys playing with others Loves to play games Talkative	Seems sure of self May be defiant Needs structured freedom May seem negative	Speaks in complete sentences Knows more than 1,500 words Asks endless questions Highly imaginative Can draw recognizable simple objects	Recites/sings the alphabet Identifies some letters Recognizes own name Knows some concepts: colors, numbers, shapes Writes some words and letters Can copy text

(continued)

Table 8.2. *continued.*

Age	Physical Development	Social Development	Emotional Development	Intellectual Development	Development as a Reader
Five Years	Hops and skips Dresses self Good balance Writes name Girls small muscle development about one year ahead of boys	Cooperative in play Has special "friends" Organized Enjoys simple games requiring turns and observing rules Wants to be a helper and have responsibilities	Self-assured Well-adjusted Home-centered Loves to be with mother Likes to help Likes to follow the rules	Creates and tells long stories Follows two to three part directions Knows the alphabet Recognizes many letters Reads own name Counts to ten Asks meaning of words Knows colors	Identifies all or most alphabet letters sounds May read ten words or more Developing a sight word inventory Can answer simple questions about a story Uses pictures as well as context clues from the rest of the sentence to figure out the meaning of a story Writes thoughts and ideas phonetically

Literacy: Most literacy assessments are exploring your child's read-ing readiness.

Children are not expected to be reading at this time in their develop-ment. The assessment may consist of a letter identification assess-ment and a "Concepts about Print" assessment.

Your child will be asked to:

- Identify and name the capital letters
- Demonstrate up to ten concepts about print (cover, tracking and so on.)

Cognition: Cognitive development is a child's ability to understand concepts. The abilities to solve problems, to remember, to se-quence, to interpret shapes and symbols, and to recognize similar-ities and differences are all indicators of cognitive development.

The main purpose of a kindergarten screening is to identify students who may have had limited exposure to literature and limited under-standing of written text. If you have followed the ideas expressed in this book, you will be pleasantly surprised in your child's success at his or her screening.

BASIC CHECKLIST FOR HOME:

_____ Ability to recite alphabet
_____ Letter name knowledge
_____ Capital letters
_____ Lowercase letters
_____ Color identification (red, blue, green, yellow, orange, purple, pink, and white)
_____ Shape identification (circle, square, and triangle)
_____ Expressive language development (Do they speak in sentences? Can they tell a story? Can they answer simple questions?)
_____ Ability to write first and last name
_____ Ability to name the letters in his or her name

_____ Follows simple three step directions

_____ Identifies the front and back cover of a book

_____ Finds the first page of a book

_____ Understands the text in a book moves from left to right

Please also refer to appendix C.

One Hundred Fantastic Children's Literature Books

PICTURE BOOKS

A Chair for My Mother by Vera B. Williams

Blueberries for Sal by Robert McCloskey

Bread and Jam for Frances by Russell Hoban

Caps for Sale by Esphyr Slobodkina

The Carrot Seed by Ruth Krauss

Corduroy by Don Freeman

Curious George by H. A. Rey

The Day Jimmy's Boa Ate the Wash by Trinka Noble

Farmer Duck by Martin Waddell

Guess How Much I Love You by Sam McBratney

Happy Birthday Moon by Frank Asch

Harold and the Purple Crayon by Crockett Johnson

Harry the Dirty Dog by Gene Zion

John Henry by Julius Lester

Joseph Had a Little Overcoat by Taback Simms

The Keeping Quilt by Patricia Polacco

The Kissing Hand by Audrey Penn

Leo, the Late Bloomer by Robert Kraus

Lyle, Lyle Crocodile by Bernard Waber

Madeline by Ludwig Bemelmans

Make Way for Ducklings by Robert McCloskey

Mike Mulligan and His Steam Shovel by Virginia Lee Burton

No, David! by David Shannon

Officer Buckle and Gloria by Peggy Rathmann

Owen by Kevin Henkes

Polar Express by Chris Van Allsburg

Round Trip by Ann Jonas

Rumpelstiltskin by Paul O. Zelinsky
The Snowy Day by Ezra Jack Keats
The Song and Dance Man by Stephen Gammell
Strega Nona by Tomie DePaola

Swimmy by Leo Lionni
The Tale of Peter Rabbit by Beatrix Potter
Three Pigs by David Wiesner
Where the Wild Things Are by Maurice Sendak

PARTICIPATION BOOKS

Animal Kisses by Barney Saltzberg
Baby's Belly Button? by Karen Katz
Dear Zoo by Rod Campbell
Moo, Baa, LA LA LA by Sandra Boynton

Pat the Bunny by Dorothy Kunhardt
The Very Quiet Cricket by Eric Carle
Where's Spot? by Eric Hill

FINGER PLAYS AND NURSERY SONGS

Frog Went a Courtin' by John Langstaff
Jamberry by Bruce Degen
Jim Aylesworth's Book of Bedtime Stories by Jim Aylesworth
My Son John by Jim Aylesworth

Over in the Meadow by John Langstaff
Peanut Butter and Jelly by Nadine Wescott
The Random House Book of Poetry for Children by Jack Prelutsky

MOTHER GOOSE

The Little Dog Laughed and Other Nursery Rhymes by Lucy Cousins

The Real Mother Goose by Blanche Fisher Wright
Sylvia Long's Mother Goose by Sylvia Long

ABC BOOKS

Chicka Chicka Boom Boom
by Bill Martin Jr.
Eating the Alphabet by Lois
Ehlert
Miss Spider's ABC by David
Kirk
*Ogres, Ogres, Ogres! Feasting
Frenzy from A to Z* by
Nicholas Heller

Old Black Fly by Jim Aylesworth
On Market Street by Arnold
Lobel
Q Is for Duck by Marcia
McClintock Folsom
Walk the Dog by Bob Barner
The Z Was Zapped by Chris Van
Allsburg

COUNTING BOOKS

Counting Kisses by Karen Katz
Five Little Monkeys by Eileen
Christelow
Seven Blind Mice by Ed Young

Ten Little Lady Bugs by Melanie
Gerth
Ten, Nine, Eight by Molly Bang

CONCEPT BOOKS

Art of Shapes by Margaret Steele
Freight Train by Donald Crews
*Is It Red? Is It Yellow? Is It Blue?
An Adventure in Color* by
Tana Hoban

Little Blue and Little Yellow by
Leo Lionni
Lunch by Denise Fleming
Mouse Paint by Ellen S. Walsh
The Tiny Seed by Eric Carle

WORDLESS BOOKS

Baby Animals: Black and White
by Phyllis Limbacher Tildes
Carl's Christmas by Alexandra
Day
Noah's Ark by Peter SpierDay

Time Flies by Eric Rohmann
*You Can't Take a Balloon into
the Metropolitan Museum* by
Jacqueline Preiss Weitzman

PREDICTABLE BOOKS

Alexander and the Terrible, Horrible, No Good, Very Bad Day by Judith Viorst

Brown Bear, Brown Bear, What Do You See? by Bill Martin Jr.

Good Night, Gorilla by Peggy Rathmann

Goodnight, Moon by Marcia Wise Brown

Green Eggs and Ham by Dr. Seuss

If You Give a Moose a Muffin by Laura Numeroff

The Little Old Lady Who Was Not Afraid of Anything by Linda Williams

Millions of Cats by Wanda Gág

One Fish, Two Fish, Red Fish, Blue Fish by Dr. Seuss

Tikki Tikki Tembo by Arlene Mosel

The Wheels on the Bus by Paul O. Zelinsky

CUMULATIVE BOOKS

The Doorbell Rang by Pat Hutchins

The Gingerbread Boy by Paul Galdone

Henny Penny by Paul Galdone

I Know an Old Lady Who Swallowed a Fly by Glen Rounds

The Mitten by Jan Brett

The Napping House by Audrey Wood

Stone Soup by Marcia Wise Brown

The Very Hungry Caterpillar by Eric Carle

CONTROLLED VOCABULARY

The Cat in the Hat by Dr. Seuss

Frog and Toad by Arnold Lobel

Rosie's Walk by Pat Hutchins

Sammy the Seal by Syd Hoff

One Hundred Great Children's Authors

Arnold, Tedd
Asch, Frank
Aylesworth, Jim
Bang, Molly
Barner, Bob
Bemelmans, Ludwig
Boynton, Sandra
Brett, Jan
Bridwell, Norman
Brown, Marc
Brown, Margaret
  Wise
Burton, Virginia Lee
Calhoun, Mary
Campbell, Rod
Carle, Eric
Christelow, Eileen
Cole, Joanna
Cousins, Lucy
Crews, Donald
Day, Alexandra
Degen, Bruce
DePaola, Tomie
Ehlert, Lois
Fleming, Denise

Folsom, Marcia
  McClintock
Fox, Mem
Freeman, Don
Gág, Wanda
Galdone, Paul
Gammell, Stephen
Gerth, Melanie
Heller, Nicholas
Henkes, Kevin
Hill, Eric
Hines, Anna
  Grossnickle
Hoban, Russell
Hoban, Tana
Hutchins, Pat
Johnson, Crockett
Jonas, Ann
Katz, Karen
Keats, Ezra Jack
Kellogg, Steven
Kirk, David
Kraus, Robert
Krauss, Ruth
Kunhardt, Dorothy

Langstaff, John
Lester, Helen
Lester, Julius
Lionni, Leo
Lobel, Arnold
London, Jonathan
Long, Sylvia
Martin Jr., Bill
Mayer, Mercer
McBratney, Sam
McCloskey, Robert
McPhail, David
Most, Bernard
Noble, Trinka H.
Numeroff, Laura
Peet, Bill
Penn, Audrey
Pilkey, Dave
Polacco, Patricia
Potter, Beatrix
Prelutsky, Jack
Rathmann, Peggy
Rey, H. A.
Rohmann, Eric
Root, Phyllis

Rounds, Glen
Rylant, Cynthia
Saltzberg, Barney
Scarry, Richard
Sendak, Maurice
Seuss, Dr.
Shannon, David
Shields, Carol
    Diggory
Simms, Taback

Slobodkina, Esphyr
Spier, Peter
Steele, Margaret
Van Allsburg, Chris
Viorst, Judith
Waber, Bernard
Waddell, Martin
Walsh, Ellen S.
Wells, Rosemary
Wescott, Nadine

Wiesner, David
Williams, Linda
Williams, Vera B.
Wood, Audrey
Wood, Don
Wright, Blanche
    Fisher
Yolen, Jane
Young, Ed
Zelinsky, Paul O.

What Do Effective Readers Do?

Good readers have strategies that they use every time they read. Before they even begin reading the story, they make connections to the main idea of the story and they set a purpose for reading. While reading, they monitor what they are reading and make predictions. After reading, they think about what they have read and look for relationships between the reading and their experiences.

Before they begin to read:

- Activate their prior knowledge about reading and the topic
- Set purposes for reading
- Determine methods for reading, according to their purposes
- Use specific prereading strategies

During their reading:

- Focus attention to the reading task
- Continuously question internally to check their own understanding
- Monitor their reading comprehension and do it so often that it becomes automatic
- Stop to use a fix-up strategy when they do not understand
- Use semantic (sentence and word meaning), syntactic (grammar), and graphophonic (written) clues to construct meanings of unfamiliar words
- Synthesize thoughts, ideas and concepts during reading
- Metacognate or talk to themselves during reading

After they finish reading:

- Evaluate their understanding of what was read
- Summarize the major ideas
- Seek additional information from outside sources
- Paraphrase the text what they have learned
- Reflect on and personalize the text
- Integrate new understandings and prior knowledge
- Use study strategies to retain new knowledge

alphabet knowledge: Recognizing the letters of the alphabet.

assessment: An assessment is a way to evaluate reading development and proficiency.

comprehension: Developing a variety of strategies to understand, remember, and communicate what is read.

concepts about print: Your child's knowledge about books: how to hold them, move from left to right, front to back.

decoding: Decoding words is the combination of phonemic awareness, letter recognition, and sound knowledge that enables us to break down new and unfamiliar words.

decoding in context: The skill of decoding combined with the reader's prior knowledge to figure out unfamiliar or unknown words.

emergent reading: The time between birth and when children begin to read and write in conventional ways.

encoding: Encoding words is the combination of phonemic awareness, letter, and sound knowledge that enables us to spell words by translating sounds into letters.

language acquisition: The stages of listening and speaking development.

language proficiency: The level at which a person can speak and understand a language.

letter identification: (*See also* alphabet knowledge) Recognizing the letters of the alphabet.

letter–sound relationship: Recognizing the letters of the alphabet and their accompanying sounds.

locomotor activity: An activity that puts the body into motion. A locomotor activity requires a person to move his or her body independently from place to place.

modeling: Showing your child how to hold a book, sound out a word, or other elements of reading by doing it for them and with them.

nonlocomotor activity: An activity that puts the body into motion but the body stays in one place.

reading fluency: The ability to read text accurately and quickly, while effectively processing meaning.

phoneme: The smallest phonetic unit in our language that is capable of passing on a distinction in meaning, as the /m/ of *mat* and the /b/ of *bat*.

phonemic awareness: Hearing and recognizing that sounds make words and that individual sounds are used to create words.

phonics: Understanding the relationships between written letters and spoken sounds, recognizing familiar words accurately and automatically, and decoding (sounding-out) new words.

prior knowledge: It is background knowledge or what the reader already knows about the subject in the reading.

sight words: Words that have been memorized. As children become aware that letters and sounds create words, they will become accustomed to seeing certain familiar words. There are published word lists of the most commonly used words in our English language. Research indicates that when a child sees a word two hundred times, it becomes part of their sight word vocabulary.

vocabulary: Learning the meaning and pronunciation of words.

Bibliography

REFERENCES

Adams, Marilyn Jager. 1994. *Beginning to Read: Thinking and Learning about Print*. Cambridge, Mass.: MIT Press.

Anderson, Richard C., E. H. Hiebert, J. A. Scott, and I. A. G. Wilkinson. 1985. *Becoming a Nation of Readers: The Report of the Commission on Reading*. Washington, D.C.: National Institute of Education.

Clay, Marie M. 1991. *Becoming Literate: The Construction of Inner Control*. Portsmouth, N.H.: Heinemann.

———. 1993. *An Observation Survey: Of Early Literacy Achievement*. Portsmouth, N.H.: Heinemann.

Committee on the Prevention of Reading Difficulties in Young Children, Commission on Behavioral and Social Sciences and Education, National Research Council. 1998. *Preventing Reading Difficulties in Young Children*, edited by Catherine E. Snow, M. Susan Burns, and Peg Griffin. Washington, D.C.: National Academy Press.

Cunningham, Patricia M. 1995. *Phonics They Use: Words for Reading and Writing*. New York: HarperCollins.

Denton, Kristin, and Jerry West. 2002. *Children's Reading and Mathematics Achievement in Kindergarten and First Grade* (PDF file), Washington, D.C.: U.S. Department of Education, National Center for Education Statistics.

Fielding, Linda G., and P. David Pearson. 1994. "Reading Comprehension: What Works." *Educational Leadership* 51 (5): 62–68.

Routman, Regie. 1994. *Invitations: Changing as Teachers and Learners K–12*. 2nd ed. Portsmouth, N.H.: Heinemann.

Stanovich, K. E. 1986. "Matthew Effects in Reading: Some Consequences of Individual Differences in the Acquisition of Literacy." *Reading Research Quarterly* 21: 360–407.

Strickland, Dorothy S. 1998. *Teaching Phonics Today: A Primer for Educators*. Newark, Del.: International Reading Association.

Teale, W. H., and E. Sulby. 1989. "Emergent Literacy: New Perspectives." In *Emerging Literacy: Young Children Learn to Read and Write*, edited by D. S. Strickland and L. M. Morrow. Newark, Del.: International Reading Association.

Yopp, Hallie Kay. 1992. "Developing Phonemic Awareness in Young Children." *Reading Teacher* 45: 696–703.

WEB RESOURCES

Bank Street College of Education. 2003. "America Reads: Early Literacy Development." Available online at www.bnkst.edu/html/americareads/early.html, [accessed January 2003].

U.S. Department of Education. 2003. "No Child Left Behind." Available online at www.nclb.gov/index.html, [accessed May 2003].

About the Author

Bonnie D. Schwartz received an M.A. in reading instruction from Concordia University in River Forest, Illinois, and is currently pursuing a doctorate in educational leadership at the University of St. Thomas in St. Paul, Minnesota. After teaching in private and public schools for nearly twenty years, Bonnie currently works for the Minnesota Department of Education as the reading content specialist and as an adjunct professor for Bemidji State University in Minnesota.